Slicing Pie

Slicing Pie

Funding Your Company Without Funds

- Version 2.3 -

Mike Moyer

Lake
Shark

ISBN 978-0615700625

This publication is designed to provide accurate and authoritative information in regard to the subject matter covered. It is sold with the understanding that the publisher is not engaged in rendering legal, accounting, or other professional service. If legal advice or other expert assistance is required, the services of a competent professional person should be sought.—*From a Declaration of Principles Jointly Adopted by a Committee of the American Bar Association and a Committee of Publishers and Associations*

All brand names and product names used in this book are trademarks, registered trademarks, or trade names of their respective holders.

Published by Lake Shark Ventures, LLC
Lake Forest, IL
www.LakeShark.com

To Anne, Anson, Merrily and Norvin

My Promise

If, after reading this book, you don't feel that it contains not just good advice, but the greatest advice on the subject that you have ever received, I will happily refund your money and apologize for wasting your time.

Mike@SlicingPie.com

My Butt-Covering Disclaimer

If anything in this book sounds like legal advice — it's not. If anything in this book sounds like financial advice — it's not. I'm not a lawyer and I'm not an accountant and I'm not a certified financial advisor.

I'm a Grunt.

For International Readers

In this book I use the term "Grunt". The word does not easily translate into other languages and cultures so I thought it might help to give you a little background before you start reading.

In the United States the term Grunt is a slang term that was originated by the military to refer to people who do hard work and are often new to their post. The term "Grunt Work" is common in US startups and businesses.

Release Notes: Version 2.3

A list of major changes for version 2.3 can be found on page 197.

One More Thing...

In this book I present a set of rules that I believe constitute fair play when it comes to dividing up equity. If you disagree with my rules as outlined here, that's fine. Make up your own rules. As long as they are fair and everyone agrees to them in advance, you should be fine.

Preface

I would like to start a business with you. I look forward to working with you to find and exploit opportunity in the market that our slow-moving competition has overlooked or is too arrogant to bother going after. I can't wait to steal their market share by creating a product or service that lures their customers away en masse.

I hope we can poach the best employees away from their day jobs or other start-ups. I'm sure their former employers will weep, but they'll get over it.

I'm sure our irreverent approach to marketing and advertising will ruffle a few feathers along the way, but that's the idea. I want our videos to go viral so we can beat those fat-cat marketing budgets from the establishment.

It's going to be fun to watch our success and see the impact we have on the market. Our competition, unable to keep up with us, will wither and die. That's okay. It's not personal—it's just business.

Before we start, however, I want to get a few things straight:

When it comes to the competition there are no holds barred. When it comes to our company and our team, however, we need to treat everyone fairly and honestly.

In business, some people may get burned. It's okay to burn the competition. It's not okay to burn each other.

Most start-up books are about breaking the rules. This one is about making them. It outlines rules of conduct about how we will treat one another when it comes to the equity in our start-up company.

Equity in the business will ultimately reward us for our individual contributions to success, when we get there. So dividing the equity fairly is critical. We need a few rules. The reason we need these rules is simple:

Fairness is More Fun.

In spite of the setbacks, the struggles, the stress, the long hours, the hard work and even the occasional failure, start-ups are fun as long as everyone participating in the start-up is treated fairly.

When everyone feels that they are getting what they deserve, everyone can get along and move the business forward as a team.

Backstabbing, greed and politicking, on the other hand, suck the fun out of a start-up faster than your company's rogue article gets deleted from Wikipedia.

Ask an old entrepreneur to reminisce about the good times and she will tell you about the high-pressure, the late nights, the victories and the defeats. Each story is exciting and inspirational. The story is always different.

Ask an old entrepreneur about the bad times and he will tell you how he was burned by a partner or an investor or a co-worker. The story is always the same.

No matter what happens in the coming months and years, I want this to be one of the good times.

So let's agree on a few basic ground rules about how to treat each other fairly before the money and emotions get in the way. I want to treat you fairly and I want to be treated fairly. That's my only agenda.

Let's begin…

Contents

Introduction

I've been an entrepreneur most of my career. I've been driven, for better or for worse, into new businesses or established businesses that want to change their old ways. And, while I am certainly interested in making enough money to buy God's summer house on Long Island, I know deep down that even without the money, there is another important measure of success.

All start-ups eventually cease being start-ups. They usually go out of business, but sometimes they turn into real companies or are bought by other companies and, thus, lose their "start-up-ness".

If the team that started the business is ready and willing to jump right back in and do it again together regardless of the outcome, then I think you have success.

Success means you do right by those who believed in you. Hopefully, at the end of your start-up, you all will laugh so hard that $100 bills squirt out your nose. But even if $100 bills don't squirt out your nose you can all get up, dust each other off, and do it again—this time older and wiser.

Slicing Pie is a short book about doing right by those who believe in you.

The Gap

Somewhere between the inception of your earth-changing idea and the investor presentation to Sequoia Capital or Andreessen Horowitz there is a gap. During that gap you are expected to have actually built something that resembles a business enough that the gentle and kind venture capitalist will decide that you have your act together and write you a fat check. I call it "the Gap" because it's during this time that you either fill the gap with behaviors that create a business or let it consume you and your wonderful idea. Most fledgling businesses experience the latter.

The days of back-of-the-envelope deals are over. (In fact, they may never have actually existed.) Few investors are willing to provide capital to a company that is little more than a rough idea.

Nowadays you need to have something worth investing in which often means a management team, a business plan, and, if you're smart, a working prototype. For bonus points get a few beta customers who are actually paying you. Now you have something worth discussing.

Putting those things together takes time and resources and, in many cases, time and resources cost money. And as you are probably aware, money is hard to come by. Sometimes the Gap is short, in other cases it is long. In all cases your idea will either show signs of becoming a business or it won't.

Lucky for you, you have a tool that is a great substitute for money when you're in a pinch. It's called equity and it can help you fill the Gap and create a business starting with nothing.

Equity in a start-up company has virtually no value. There is no real market for start-up equity trading and you can't buy food or clothing with it. In most cases individuals can't sell it to other individuals and even if you find a willing buyer the government has all sorts of rules regulating who can and can't invest (more later on the JOBS act).

In spite all of these obvious shortcomings you can still use equity to acquire many of the things you need. Building a business using equity is a powerful and exciting option. It's a beautiful thing.

Equity in your start-up company can be used to pay employees, hire consultants, buy supplies and even pay rent. However, because it has no real value you will have to (1) convince people that it will have a lot of value in the future and (2) provide a logical explanation of how you calculated the amount of equity you are giving them.

When you use equity to compensate people you need to make sure you are fair and equitable. This can be like walking a tightrope. Doing it wrong could lead to a quick end to your business and your relationships with those involved. It can also cause irreparable damage to your professional credibility and wind up costing you real money. Do it right and the world is your oyster.

Interestingly, little has been written about the process of using equity to build a business. It is a process that trips up even the savviest entrepreneurs. Ask a dozen people and you'll get a dozen answers.

There are a plethora of great books about starting companies and bootstrapping and raising money and marketing and all those great things that can help your business grow. But as far as I know there is only one book about how to use equity to get your start-up off the ground and you're holding it.

That Little Awkward Conversation

I've seen it before and I'll see it again. A couple of people have a great idea for a new business. They get excited. They start hashing out the details. They build a prototype and speak with a few potential customers. The idea starts taking shape so they put together a business plan and a tidy little investor presentation. Then they start thinking about quitting their jobs and how they are going to spend all the oodles and oodles of cash that is going to start rolling in.

Everything looks great and then, out of nowhere, the topic of equity comes up. It's been on their minds, but they put off the discussions because they don't know what to do. The conversation looks something like this:

"We need to think about how we should split up the company, you know, the stock or shares or whatever," says start-up guy one.

"Uh-huh," replies start-up guy two.

"Well, we need to do it because I'm getting my lawyer-brother-in-law to set up the corporation for us. He's doing it for free but we need to pay the filing fee," says start-up guy one.

"Um, okay," says start-up guy two. "What do you want to do, I mean, how should we split it up?"

"I'm not quite sure; I thought we could talk about it," answers start-up guy one.

"Okay, yeah, that's a good idea. Maybe we should split it 30/70," suggests start-up guy two.

"Right, I think that's fair, it was my idea so 70% seems about right for me," start-up guy one agrees.

"Um, well, I thought *I* would take 70% and you would be the 30% because I'm the developer and I'm doing all the work right now," says start-up guy two.

"Oh, err, you are doing a lot right now, but when the product is done I'll be doing most of the work and it was my idea," replies start-up guy one with a little frustration.

"Yeah, but there will still be a lot of upkeep on the program and we're using my hosting account so I think it's only fair that I should get more," says start-up guy two.

"Dude! That's not fair; you wouldn't even *be* here if it weren't for me. *I* should get more than you," snaps start-up guy one.

"Dude! You couldn't do this thing at all without me because you don't know how to code. Besides, *I* added all the bells and whistles, your idea wouldn't have worked the way you wanted it!" yells start-up guy two.

"That's not true! *I* came up with the great idea, *you* only thought of a little bit. *I* can get another developer in a heartbeat, *your* skills are replaceable!" yells start-up guy one.

And so it goes. Tensions rise, arguments ensue and the relationship starts deteriorating. Even if it goes better than in this example, it's a weird conversation at best. Everything else is great, but this one little conversation seems to create an unwanted awkwardness. It's a palpable break in the "start-up high," that wonderful feeling you get when you embark on a new venture with people who think like you. You are one with the idea and the idea is one with you. But this little conversation seems to create a weird tension. If you could just get over it, you would be well on your way to acquiring Google in a hostile takeover in year three.

The Disgruntled Millionaire

Not long ago I had lunch with a man who had recently become a millionaire after the company he worked for was sold for hundreds of millions of dollars. He was an early employee and was now rich beyond his wildest dreams.

In spite of his financial gain, the man was complaining about the deal. He said that while he was happy that he now had a nice nest egg, he would have gotten a lot more if he hadn't been "screwed" by the company's owner. While he made only a few million dollars the company's owner had made over one hundred million dollars.

His resentment can be traced back to the early days of the business when early equity was being allocated. He didn't feel that he received a percent of the equity that properly reflected his contribution.

Wow, I thought, here is a man who four years ago was headed towards retirement on social security and a meager pension. He is now a millionaire and can retire in style, yet all he can think about is how he resents the man who helped put him there. I'm sure he will get over it and move on, but it's a shame that such a happy time should be sullied by resentment and anger.

This scenario plays out time and time again. A new company hits it big and interpersonal relationships become strained because many people feel undervalued. The biggest wins go to the people with the largest equity stake in the company. Of course, not *every* employee deserves equity; but, very early participants often feel entitled, especially if they see concrete evidence of their contribution. There are movies about this kind of thing.

After the deal, the participants usually go their separate ways if they don't feel they were treated fairly. This is unfortunate because they are the people who should stay and try again. After all, they had one successful deal, why not create another?

As a rule, people expect to be treated fairly. They expect their contribution will not only be valued, but also rewarded in a manner that is consistent with the rewards of others. Nothing causes more damage to business relationships than when there is a perception of unfair or inconsistent compensation and reward practices.

In my experience I've found that it's not really about the money. It's frustrating how often people think money is a motivator. It's very difficult to refute, but I know that money is only a part of the equation. People want to know that their contribution is important and valued. And, they want some kind of evidence that that is the case. They want proof that they are a valued contributor on the team.

A Falling Out

Whenever I hear of two people in a business relationship that have a "falling out" I usually start looking for the answer to the question "who burned whom?"

When a falling out occurs it generally means that at least one person in the relationship didn't feel as if they were treated fairly. And, rather than coming to an equitable agreement, they simply stopped working together. Both leave the relationship angrily trying to justify why the other person was wrong. Even in situations that the individuals would describe as "amicable", there is usually anger and resentment.

In many cases burning a fellow entrepreneur isn't intentional; it is a byproduct of ignorance rather than a product of arrogance.

The life of an entrepreneur, especially a career entrepreneur, can be exciting and meaningful. Entrepreneurs spend their careers, or at least part of their careers, trying to improve people's lives. Not just the lives of their customers, but also the lives of their employees and, of course, their investors. I think entrepreneurship is a noble profession.

According to Carl J. Schramm, former president and CEO of the Ewing Marion Kauffman Foundation, "Entrepreneurs give security to other people; they are the generators of social welfare." The country needs entrepreneurs, the world needs entrepreneurs. Without them not much would happen.

In spite of the exciting life and important role of entrepreneurs, most people never become entrepreneurs. To most people the life is too risky. Most people can't handle the ambiguity. Most people are afraid of failure. Every entrepreneur fails more often than they succeed.

Good Lessons and Bad Lessons

Failure is how an entrepreneur learns. In the start-up life there are lessons that help you become a better entrepreneur and lessons that force you to become a worse entrepreneur. Good lessons are those that stem from failure related to how you and your team ran the business.

Good lessons improve an entrepreneur's chances for future success. If you created a product that nobody wants, you will have learned to listen to customers in the future. If your marketing didn't work you will learn to communicate better in the future. If your employees leave you, you will learn to be a better manager in the future. If you run out of money, you will learn to better manage cash in the future.

If a competitor comes out of nowhere and hands you your butt on a plate, you will learn to be more mindful of the market in the future and create a brand that will insulate you from the competition.

In fact, just about any failure that comes in the normal course of creating a business will ultimately make the entrepreneur stronger. She will learn to be a better predictor and a better responder in the future. In the start-up world, this kind of failure begets success. These are good lessons.

Bad lessons, on the other hand, decrease an entrepreneur's chances for success. They generally stem from failure related to getting burned by your partners.

Being an entrepreneur requires a great amount of trust and confidence. It requires bold moves and big ideas that change the way people think about life. When entrepreneurs become less confident and less trusting effectiveness diminishes. When they get burned by their partners they do learn, but they learn bad lessons. They learn to spend more time covering their own butts. They learn to spend more time and money writing contracts and agreements. They learn to move more slowly and take fewer risks. They learn to be less like entrepreneurs and more like everyone else.

It is demoralizing when entrepreneurs are burned by people they thought they could trust. It saps their confidence. They feel stupid and become bitter. Worse yet, their families lose confidence in them and become less supportive.

Inasmuch as failure is inevitable for entrepreneurs, getting burned is also inevitable. However, getting burned doesn't *have* to be part of the equation and I believe there are very positive and productive ways to mitigate the long-term damage.

Equity- A Root Cause

Unfair equity allocation is a root cause of perceived mistreatment that can destroy relationships. In some cases founders *deliberately* take advantage of their partners, but in most cases the problem is accidental. The founder makes mistakes and it appears as if they burned their partners even though that wasn't the intent. As in the case of the disgruntled millionaire example, the *intent* of the founder was to treat everyone fairly. However, because of a few bad decisions early on, there was a perception of deliberate injustice.

Partners and Equity

When two or more people form a partnership it is because they want to share the risk of a new venture. If I hire you to clean my house, we are not partners. I am your employer and you are my employee. If I ask you to be my partner it implies we are going to work together in some way to build value and reap the benefits later on. For instance, I can partner with you to clean someone else's house and we can split the money somehow.

The problem is that because we get paid when the job is complete, we work for nothing until it's over. So, as we clean we are essentially building equity in an asset (clean house) that will eventually be converted to cash when the owner of the house pays us. The owner gets the clean house and we get our money. So the question is, how much do we each get?

"How much do we each get?" is the most dangerous question of all business questions. It causes more problems than any other question I have found. It is most dangerous in situations where the contribution of the individual has a material impact on the outcome.

Here is what I mean: in the above example, the housecleaning partners have to figure out how to split the money. This decision, more than any other decision they will make, will determine the ongoing quality of their relationship. Doing this right is really hard.

Let's say we decide to "keep it simple" and split the money "50/50". I show up with a bucket full of cleaning supplies that cost me about $15, you show up with nothing. I work hard for three hours cleaning the kitchen and the bathrooms and you sweep the hall. The job pays $50. I get $25 which, after I subtract the cost of the supplies, nets me $10. You get $25—all profit for hardly any work. Hmmmm…this doesn't seem fair. (By the way, 50/50 splits are extremely common and extremely problematic.)

Let's say we decide to determine the split *after* we get paid. I think I deserve $10 for the supplies, plus $5 for my time in getting the supplies, plus $5 for getting the gig and $10 an hour for my work. So, after three hours of work I think I should get the whole $50. You think that compensating me for my supplies is fair, but you also think it's only worth $1 because there are supplies left over. Plus, you want $20 an hour because you have more cleaning experience than I do. At the end of the day we have an issue that can't be solved very amicably.

So what happens? In either case the relationship deteriorates and we will either have to solve our differences or split up.

Sometimes you luck out. If we both brought our own supplies and we both did our fair share of the work we would both be happy with $25. As long as we keep doing our fair share, life is good. But what if you get sick? What if I get tired of cleaning houses? What if I stop caring? What if your sister wants to join us? What if, what if, what if?

Partnerships are fragile relationships. Many of them fail because of the partners' inability to answer the question of how much do we each get?

Equity Allocation

Equity is ownership in an asset. An asset is something that produces cash or can be converted into cash by selling it at a later date. (Nobody wants equity in a liability which is something that consumes cash.) So when you own equity in something you have a right to the future cash it produces. It's pretty simple- right?

The problem with equity is that it can be very difficult to value because most of us can't predict the future. Some of us are better at it than others, but at the end of the day the future is all based on assumptions. Businesses operate on a complex set of assumptions, some of which are grounded in historical trends. Start-up businesses are pretty much all wild guesses.

If I own a lemonade stand how much is it worth? The stand itself and the supplies may have cost $100, but that doesn't mean I can sell it for $100. If it's hot I may be able to sell $100 worth of lemonade, but that doesn't mean it's not going to rain.

So, I have to make some assumptions. I'm going to assume that I can sell the equipment and supplies for about what similar stands are selling on Ebay.com- $50 for the stand and $20 for the supplies. Next, I check the weather and it gives a 20% chance of rain. So, I'm going to take that into account and bet that I'll make $80. I'll use up the supplies so they won't be around to sell later. I'll call the stand worth $50 + $80 or $130. That's how much the stand is worth in the next 24 hours. As you can see, there are a lot of factors. If I want you to be my partner, we're going to have to work through these scenarios and agree on which one we like. There are no guarantees. I may not be able to sell on Ebay, it might rain, or I might get robbed- who knows?

Let's say I don't own the stand. You do. Then it doesn't matter how much it's worth as long as I get paid what I earn. But, sometimes you will want to pay me based on the performance of the business which is a combination of my sales skills plus your equipment. You could pay me on commission, but you would rather reinvest the money into the business.

One way to get me to work without giving me cash is to allocate some of the equity to me. You are allocating a percent of the rights to the future cash the business generates either by selling lemonade or by selling the stand and supplies.

By accepting equity instead of cash I am assuming the risk that I might never get paid. So, I'm going to accept equity (future cash) that I believe will be worth more than what I would otherwise get paid now (current cash). Figuring this out, even for a simple lemonade stand, is complicated.

This book outlines a simpler, more accurate and more fair solution that doesn't require a complex set of assumptions or a crystal ball. This doesn't have to be a guessing game.

How I Hope You Will Use this Book

This book is designed to help alleviate that awkward little conversation that, if handled improperly, can create a rift in your little blossoming company that may never be overcome. It is designed to create a common understanding between you and your partners and your early employees. It is designed to help you make the right decisions at the get-go.

I hope, that when you bring on a new

person or partner or vendor, you will hand them a copy of this book and say, "here, this is how we're going to split the equity until we raise our first round of financing." Bang—the awkward conversation is addressed and tackled.

Using this book as a guideline for how you will pay people with equity in your company will save you a lot of time and a lot of anxiety. It will reward you and your team for hard work and, in the long run, it will make sure everyone gets what they deserve. That's it, simple as pie.

Boy, I wish someone had handed me this book when I joined or started probably a dozen businesses over the past twenty years. That would have saved me a lot of headaches.

I've created this book because *I* wanted a book *I* could hand to someone before they got involved with one of my businesses. I needed this book to solve my own business problems. In fact, as I write, I have two businesses on my mind that are facing exactly the issues that this book is designed to address. I figured I can hash it out separately with each one of them or I can write a little book about it and share it with you.

Pie A La Mode

House Cleaning

To see the solution to the housecleaning problem, visit **SlicingPie.com** and click on the Pie à la Mode or scan the code.

Will work for pie.

Chapter One:

Slicing Pie

Allocating equity, otherwise known as "Slicing the Pie" is tricky. And, as we've discussed so far, it can not only cause irreparable damage to otherwise important business relationships, but also it can prevent an otherwise good business from even getting started in the first place. In order to understand how to slice the pie, you first need to understand a few things about the pie itself. Unlike apple pies, equity pies can grow and grow and grow.

All Pie is Created Equal

In the beginning, all pies are worth nothing. They start out as just an idea. Some guy is sitting at his desk or on the subway, or in bed, or in the car, or in the shower, or on a plane, or in the hall, or at lunch or somewhere else and his mind wanders; he thinks about a problem and a clever solution.

So clever, in fact, that he begins to think it would make a great business. The more he thinks about the clever idea, the more convinced he becomes that there is money to be made. He gets excited. And, before long, he is convinced that he is only a few short years away from early retirement.

If you remember nothing from this book, remember this: all pies, and therefore equity, are worth *nothing* when they are first created. Pies are essentially ideas and ideas are pretty much worthless in the beginning.

All too often a would-be entrepreneur is so convinced that her idea is going to be "the next big thing" that she locks it away, telling no one for fear it will be stolen. I've seen it time and time again. Someone will allude to a great idea and get all weird and secretive when you ask them about it.

I once knew a guy who kept an idea for a new kind of paintbrush secret for years. Finally, after much prodding, he told me about it. "Cool," I said. I told him that I knew some guys who could help develop it a little further and he agreed to let me talk about it. The next week I came back with a working prototype of the brush and it worked exactly as described.

Now all he needed to do was manufacture it, buy inventory, create a fulfillment operation, create a brand, marketing plan, build a sales force, raise money and a million other things that the idea needed in order for it to become valuable. I guess he didn't want to do those things because the idea still remains a prototype, locked in a closet somewhere. By the way, I'm not trying to be critical here. Like most people he has better or more important things to do than build a paintbrush company from scratch.

Occasionally companies pay for ideas; however, payment is generally in the form of a royalty payment with some kind of advance. Royalties recognize the importance of an idea in a start-up by providing payments upon the successful implementation of the idea. I'll cover how to use royalties later, just keep in mind that rarely, if ever, does a company pay, in advance, for a back-of-the-napkin concept alone. The idea has to have a little meat on the bones in the form of a market analysis, prototype, business plan, or patent. In these cases they aren't buying the idea, they are buying the opportunity of which the idea is a part.

Ideas, if you must assign a value to them, are worth about a dime a dozen. They don't become worth anything until they get baked into pies. Next, if after baking the pie, you find that people are willing to pay for the idea and you find that you can produce it for less than they are willing to pay, then (and only then) have you built value.

Sure there are stories about the guy who invented the little plastic thing pizza shops use to keep the box from squishing the pizza that made millions.

Or, you've heard the one about the woman who invented the "thingamabob" and retired to Hawaii. Those stories are either urban legends or exceedingly rare. Either way odds are they won't happen to your idea.

How Pie is Valued

Putting a value on a company (pie) is much more art than science. For established companies, investors use a variety of tools. The most popular indicators of value have to do with cash flow, revenue and earnings.

People buy pies because they are assets or the buyer thinks it will become an asset. An asset is something that produces income.

The value of the pie is based primarily on the amount of income it is able to generate. Because the future is uncertain there is a lot of speculation with regard to future income generation so the value of a pie can vary dramatically based on who is looking at it.

If your company does not generate income you may be able to estimate a resale value based on the underlying assets of a company such as buildings, machines, inventory, etc. This is useful when the company doesn't currently generate income or if the owners think the income is less than the resale value.

Most of the early-stage deals I know of focus on income vs. assets. Especially for tech companies that usually don't have any real assets.

Cash-Out

At any given time, your company is worth whatever you can sell it for. If my lemonade stand consistently generates $1,000 profit per year I may decide that, rather than waiting a year to get the $1,000, I'd rather have some money right now.

So, I find someone who thinks that they would like to run a lemonade stand for a living and take home $1,000 per year or more if they think they can hawk lemonade better than I can. I tell them that the company is worth $5,000 because I think the market will not change much or even improve (global warming might make people thirstier) over the next five years so profits should stay the same. They think the market will change (Jamba Juice down the street) and so they offer $3,000. I say okay. They just bought my pie for $3,000. I take the money and run.

In this case they just bought the whole pie from me and I *cashed-out*, meaning I took the money out of the business. The pie now belongs to someone else. My share of the pie is 0% and the buyer's share is 100%. This transaction is also known as an "exit".

Investors are always talking about exit strategies because they want to know how they are going to cash out of the business and take a return on their investment. In fact, all equity owners want to know the circumstances under which their equity will be cashed out.

Cashing-out is also useful when you want to disconnect someone from the business. If I own 90% of the business and you own 10% of the business and we agree that the value of the business is $100 I could give you $10 and take your shares. Thus, you turned your shares into cash and are now cashed-out.

It is not uncommon to cash-out shareholders who have small amounts of equity and are no longer involved in the business.

Cash-In

In many (most) cases a company will want to raise working capital. In this case they want to sell a part of the pie but keep the *cash in* the business and retain part of the ownership themselves. This is a very typical scenario. When you put cash in a business in exchange for equity it helps set a benchmark for the company's value. Whatever the investor paid for equity is a generally considered a good indicator of what the rest of the world will say it is worth.

For instance, if an investor buys 50% of the pie for $1,000,000 the pie is now "worth" $2,000,000 as long as the money stays in the business instead of being passed on to the original shareholders. So, now the pie is bigger.

The founders were able to convince an investor that the original pie was worth $1 million (this is called a "pre-money" valuation), the investor put in another $1 million, so now it is "worth" $2 million- get it? If you had half of the original pie your piece was valued at $500,000. Now you have 25% of the pie and it is still worth $500,000.

If a few months later someone buys half the company for $3,000,000 in the next round of financing, now the whole pie is worth $6,000,000.

The original pie, before the investment, had grown to be worth $3,000,000. Now your share, which was 25% of the original pie, or 12.5% of the new pie, is worth $750,000. Your equity stake has dropped from 25% to 12.5% but the value has grown to $750,000.

At the end of the day, the cash value of your equity is much more interesting than your percent ownership. Notice that while your percentage is shrinking, your wealth is growing.

It is funny how often people lose sight of this simple concept. Pies get bigger and bigger as value grows. Equity grows and grows. People who think equity is a finite resource are wrong. I once worked for a guy who was so paranoid about giving up "all the equity" that he couldn't sleep. He was a fool.

As long as a people are willing to pay more and more for your company's equity the value of your shares will also grow, regardless of what percent ownership they represent.

Of course there are situations where companies *lose* value in which case you lose value too. If the next guy invested $1,000,000 for half the company instead of $3,000,000 the company would be worth $2,000,000 and your 12.5% share would be worth $250,000.

Sometimes the company issues different "classes" of equity that might dilute the value of your shares. There are a number of possibilities that are beyond the scope of this book. There are people who make a nice living figuring out stuff like this- I'm not one of them.

The moral of the story: concentrate on building value and don't worry about percentage ownership. Don't get hung up on it. Pies can grow beyond your wildest dreams. If you don't think so, think about Google, Microsoft, Groupon, Facebook and Apple.

It doesn't really matter what you think the company might be worth someday. What matters is that people are treated fairly and they ultimately get a payout that's fair given what they put in.

Sometimes pies grow- this is good.

Paying with Pie

Remember that "Gap" period I mentioned earlier? If you have no money, you can pay people with pie.

Using pie during the Gap means you will have to convince people that the pie has value before there are any real benchmarks. To do this you will have to be able to convince people that your business idea is great and that you (with their help) will be able to turn it into some cold hard cash in the not-too-distant future.

It is important to note, before we continue, that while paying with pie can be a great way to get your business off the ground and through the Gap, you must be careful not to make too many slices. In general, investors want to invest in a pie that is relatively intact. If it's not, it will be less attractive. Investors want to see that all of the shareholders are actively involved in the business. While this is not always possible when you pay with pie, we will go over some ways to keep the pie relatively intact.

The other thing you will have to do is find people who are willing to work for pie instead of cash. Not everyone is willing to assume the risk that they will never get paid. However, I think you will find that a lot of people will take pie over cash if they think they are going to be part of an exciting new venture.

There is a word for people who will take pie instead of cash: "Grunts."

Grunts

Grunts are people who are willing to forgo cash compensation in exchange for a piece of the pie. Grunts do the work necessary to turn an idea into a reality. They will do the fun work and the dirty work. They are as comfortable licking stamps as they are building a strategic plan.

Grunts ask for little in return- usually just pie. They can generally survive in sub-standard habitats. They have been known to thrive in garages, basements and spare bedrooms. They can be found lurking in coffee shops, college campuses and even within the cubicles and offices of a day job.

Grunts don't need much. They are highly resourceful. They can act on scant little information and leap tall problems in a single bound. They are motivated by the dream of success.

Grunts are pack animals. They travel in herds. Rarely can a Grunt do all the work themselves so they offer some of the pie to other Grunts. If you can win the heart of a good Grunt, your idea will become a reality as long as you treat the Grunt with respect and fair play.

Grunts come for the pie

Baking Pies

In order to make tasty pie you need the right ingredients. These will be provided by Grunts. You, by the way, are a Grunt too. While the type of ingredients and amount of each will vary depending on the flavor of pie you are baking, the basic ingredients are as follows:

Time

Time is probably the most significant ingredient that a Grunt has to offer. Many people don't have a lot of money, but they have time, especially early in their career or if the previous pies they helped make didn't sell or grow the way they had hoped.

Grunts dedicate time turning ideas into pies. Not all time is created equal. The time of the experienced chief technology officer is worth more than the junior programmer. However, both people need to be treated fairly. If you have the right Grunts in the herd you will be fine.

Ideas

Grunts are a fountain of ideas for products, ideas for marketing, ideas for sales, ideas for operations. Good employees come to the table with lots and lots of good ideas. Remember, however, that an idea by itself usually has little or no value. It has to be made into pie first.

Relationships

All companies need relationships that can turn
into customers, investors, partners or advisors.
Sometimes relationships are built through the
operation of the business and sometimes an
employee brings pre-existing relationships with
him or her to the table. Existing relationships can
really accelerate the process and finding people
who have these relationships is an important part
of the process.

Intellectual Property

Patents, trademarks and other ways of doing
things are intellectual property. As long as the
individual has a legal right to use these assets they
can be an important part of a fledgling business,
especially when it comes to creating strategic
advantages.

When a person joins a company and
allows them to use their IP, the company should
provide a fair slice of pie in return for a license to
use the IP.

Funds

You can use pie to acquire a lot of the ingredients
you need for your start-up company, but not
everything. Try buying stamps with pie. I'm pretty
sure the postman will look at you like you are
crazy. So you can put "stamps" on your list of
hundreds of things that you probably can't get

with pie. So, sooner or later you will need to get your hands on some money. Money comes in the form of cash, loans and credit (which is similar to a loan).

Cash

Cash comes in the form of early working capital or covered expenses for which reimbursement is not expected. This is different than a significant angel or venture capital investment. This is money that helps get the business off the ground.

When you attract significant money the game changes. More on this later.

Loans

Loans from an individual to the company that are *expected to be repaid.*

Or…

Loans from a bank to the company to finance the purchase or operations of the company.

Credit

Credit comes in the form of personal credit card debt or company loans that an employee had to personally guarantee.

Supplies and Equipment

Business-facilitating supplies and equipment are pencils, paper, personal computers or other items that make the business easier to operate efficiently.

The test here is whether the business could operate at all without them. Many Grunts, for example, use their own personal laptops during the formation-stages of a business. This is an example of equipment that *facilitates* the business. This is different than supplies and equipment without which the business couldn't exist.

Business-enabling supplies and equipment such as data servers, printing presses, delivery vans or other items without which the business would not be a business in the first place.

For instance, if a couple of dudes are starting a pizza shop and one of them provides a pizza oven, that would be an example of a business-enabling piece of equipment.

There is often a fine line between whether supplies and equipment is business-facilitating or business-enabling. It's often a judgment call. Take chairs, for instance. An employee shouldn't expect her $1000 Herman Miller Aeron chair to be considered a business-enabling piece of equipment even though you need chairs. In most cases a $25 used office chair will serve the same purpose.

Facilities

Facilities that would otherwise generate income for the owner, include office buildings, retail locations, studio space or other facilities that the owner would typically rent out if the start-up wasn't using it.

In this case the owner has an opportunity cost of dedicating the asset to baking the pie.

If all the employees work out of a spare room in one of their houses, this wouldn't count because the person probably isn't planning on renting out the spare room in his house. If you and the other employees are a bunch of slobs, you may want to throw him or her a bone in exchange for using the spare room and making a mess.

Other Resources

Some Grunts may have access to resources that your company can use from time to time, company won't actually own. For instance, a Grunt may have employees from another company that can work on your company's projects on a part-time basis. Or, perhaps a Grunt has some equipment that your company can "rent" with pie.

While some ingredients are more productive than others, *all* should be treated as if they build positive value.

Why, you might ask, should I treat them all as if they build positive value? Because it's not fair not to. If you are paying with pie you have to be fair. If a person does work on behalf of a company and that work turns out to be a waste of time you still got value. Specifically, you learned that that particular activity was a waste of time and you can avoid it in the future.

A friend of mine (a Grunt), grunted away for a guy for almost two years and followed the direction of the controlling partner. One day, on a whim, the controlling partner decided to abandon the original strategy in favor of another one. He fired my friend and took back all the equity because his work was not related to the new strategy. How could he have known? Ask yourself: is this fair?

Not all effort is productive, but it all counts

When a herd of Grunts agrees to dedicate their time, energy and resources towards a problem, it is impossible to tell, in advance, if it is going to work. It is not fair to judge the value of the inputs using the benefit of hindsight.

This makes a lot of seasoned entrepreneurs uncomfortable. After all, value creation is essential in any business. The more experience you have the more you can see, with 20/20 hindsight, where value was created. Many people mistake their ability to have good hindsight with their ability to have good foresight.

If this is you, take a break and think about how you might identify value creation before it happens. It's pretty hard, even for smart people. (Hint: some Grunts have better track records than other Grunts. These Grunts should be allocated more pie because of what they are capable of because not all Grunts are created equal).

Start-up companies are risk-taking entities. By devaluing an individual Grunt's input based on hindsight, you are asking that Grunt to assume the risk on behalf of the herd. You cannot allow a single Grunt to bear the burden of risk for the herd- it's not fair.

When there is a pie, Grunts will show up and help make the pie grow. A Grunt is happy sharing the pie with other Grunts as long as he or she was treated fairly in the process. In the end there will be enough for everyone if things go right. After all, there is virtually no end to how big the pie can grow. If your company fails the

Grunt will try again someday as long as they were treated fairly.

If you have been an entrepreneur or worked for an early-stage start-up filled with Grunts, you know there are few places on earth with more excitement, energy and passion. A herd of Grunts is a sight to be seen and a force to be reckoned with. When a Grunt is not in a herd, they are often pre-occupied with trying to find one or trying to build one. Sometimes Grunts join a number of herds. Herds of Grunts are great

The Proper Care and Feeding of Grunts

As I said before, Grunts don't ask for much. You can pay them in pie, or at least partly in pie. They also need to feel as if they are part of the herd. Grunts thrive on their inclusion in the herd. That means their opinions are taken seriously and their contribution is valued.

It is important to feed a Grunt the right amount of pie. If you don't feed a Grunt enough pie, they will feel undervalued and they might leave the herd. If you feed a Grunt too much pie, the other Grunts may feel undervalued, give up and leave the herd. Or worse, they will feel undervalued, give up and *stay*.

When employees give up and stay, the environment becomes plagued with resentment and low morale. Trust me when I say that these emotions are start-up killers.

Using equity to compensate contributors, or slicing pie, can be one of the most important tools for attracting and maintaining a healthy herd of hard working Grunts when it is done right. When it's done wrong you will have a lot of disgruntled Grunts.

As a Grunt myself, I've been the member and, in some cases, the leader of many herds. I have been in very few herds where all the members of the herd were fed properly.

I have also been in herds where I've been fed more than my fair share and I have been in herds where I have been fed less than my fair share. In all cases the relationships I had with other employees was strained because of the inequity.

When people slice pie they usually do it wrong. They make one of two mistakes. They either slice the pie *before* they bake it or they slice the pie *after* they bake it.

Before it's Baked

The most common mistake entrepreneurs make is slicing the pie before it is baked. In my experience this is what about 90% of people do. They "do the deal" with one another up front because they think it will avoid arguments later on. This is rarely the case. There is always an argument. It may be one-sided and you may never hear about it because the other person left in a huff.

I was once in a business with a guy who didn't understand the concept of growing pies.

He thought equity was a finite resource as many people do. So, he set out to slice the pie for every possible Grunt that might come along. He was the worst slicer I have ever come across. Needless to say, I don't work with him anymore and I won't ever join a herd that he is in. He is a successful guy, but he just doesn't understand start-up pie very well so his ill-gotten success is built at the expense of others.

When Grunts succeed they should succeed together, when they fail, they should fail together.

The reason that slicing pie *before* baking pie causes so many problems is that start-ups change fast—really fast. You never know what is around the corner and it is impossible to anticipate what will happen. So, when things inevitably change, you and your fellow Grunts will have to endure painful renegotiations to set things right, or live with the inequity of the split. Either way relationships will suffer, sometimes beyond repair.

I've made the slicing before mistake more than once in my life and I've always regretted it. Several years ago I had an idea for a web site that was destined to change the world. I was over-eager to get it started so I made the mistake of slicing the pie before I baked it. I gave a developer 75% of the equity to build the site. I kept 25% which was fine with me because I had planned on being a silent partner. Now it's built…

In order for it to have any value, however, we need to market it. I'm a marketing guy; but, as a minority shareholder I have little motivation to dedicate my time to the project. I burned myself by slicing the pie in advance.

The developer is unfairly burned too. He's a great developer, but he doesn't do marketing. If we want to hire another Grunt to do the marketing work what do we do? Should I spend time finding someone and paying them out of my pocket? Should I put additional time in? Should the developer?

Our ownership is fixed. Maybe we can give the new marketing guy a chunk of the equity but who will give up their pie? Remember, the pie is pretty much the same size as when we started. We have a web site, but without paying customers it's not worth much.

Should I give up more of my pie or should the developer give up his? Should we each give up the same amount of pie or do we give up in proportion with our shares? It's a tough question and a tough conversation.

Even if we can work through it, it will take its toll on our relationship and it will certainly come up again before we're done. I could suggest, for instance, that we start over and reallocate the pie. He will undoubtedly have less which will be annoying for him even though he knows that his current stake is worthless anyway. At the end of the day, the momentum and excitement has been sucked out of the business because of bad pie slicing. Renegotiation can be a company-killer.

You might think I would have learned

from this mistake. Nope. Not long after I had another idea for a new company and bounced it off a few developers. I tried to entice them into doing the development work by offering them pie. They are Grunts so they happily agreed. Again, I made the mistake of slicing the pie before the pie had been baked.

When I realized that the technology component was much smaller than I had anticipated I realized I had offered too much pie for development. Now I have developers who think they own a huge hunk of my concept and neither of them have done any work whatsoever! That project is now stalled for two reasons: First, I sliced the pie in advance and now I have to renegotiate with them and, second, I stopped working on the project because it gave me the idea for this book!

I will not make this mistake again!

Vesting and Options

Vesting is a popular hedging method for those who slice the pie before baking it. Vesting is a structure under which your equity is granted according to a certain schedule. For instance, the company may give you 2,000 shares in the company with 100 shares vesting at the end of each month. At the end of the eighth month you would own 800. At the end of 20 months you would own all 2,000 shares. After that you have to either get nothing or negotiate more shares.

People figure if they slice up the pie and

allow it to vest over time they create a safety net if the Grunt doesn't work out. The problem is that you have to predetermine the amount of pie a Grunt will receive which means you are also trying to predetermine the value of that pie. This just doesn't work during the Gap phase of a start-up. However, as a company matures the value is more concrete and a vesting program can work nicely.

Companies like vesting because they think it helps retain employees. The employee has to stay a certain number of months, for instance, before their equity vests. If the employee leaves they stop vesting.

Vesting and options are legitimate solution for slicing pie and it works reasonably well. Later in this book I'll tell you how to talk to your lawyer about setting up Grunt Fund-style vesting.

Along with vesting, it is customary for businesses to use options rather than actual equity. Options allow the Grunt to reap the financial rewards associated with equity, but avoid some of the tax implications. When you use options you are essentially keeping track of how you will slice the pie when it's time to eat. It keeps the pie whole and it keeps your knife clean.

A Note about Vesting

When appropriate, the rules outlined in this book can serve as the basis for a vesting schedule. This will help address potential tax issues that arise from issuing equity. More later on this…

After it's Baked

Sometimes entrepreneurs anticipate the problems with slicing pie *before* baking the pie so they decide to slice the pie *after* they bake it. This is even worse than doing it in advance. Now that the pie is baked and has some value there will be a Grunt feeding frenzy with every Grunt trying to get the biggest piece they can get. And, to make matters worse, they are starving! They haven't been fed yet!

Some friends of mine once started a bike shop. They all put time and energy into it and, lo and behold, they made money!

So they had a pile of cash and none of them knew what to do with it. Who did it belong to? Did they keep it in the company or split it up? Some guys did more work than other guys, plus some had spent some of their own money for marketing materials.

One guy owned all the tools and the stand. One guy was a member of the bike club and a lot of the members were customers. After much ado, they chickened-out and split the money evenly. They all felt burned. The business was over.

When you slice a pie after it is baked you are forced to make judgment calls on each other's contribution. You have to recreate what worked and what didn't work while you were baking the pie. Everyone has a different point of view so nobody agrees.

Sometimes a herd of Grunts will do a little bit of work, like writing a business plan, before they start thinking about slicing the pie. So, the pie starts baking and they start seeing the value and they all want their piece. Again, you get a feeding frenzy and a herd of disgruntled Grunts.

Whether you're slicing pie before or after it's baked you run a high risk of getting burned or burning someone else. It is a tightrope, even if you have the best intentions.

Sometimes entrepreneurs find the right answer because they have enough experience to know what they will need, sometimes they luck out, and sometimes the pie grows so big so fast that nobody cares (like during the dot-com bubble).

However, you can't always count on these things to work in your favor and good companies with good Grunts often ruin their chances for success when they make the inevitable bad choice.

Fixed-Splits

Whether people divide the pie before or after it's baked they exacerbate their problems by using a fixed split (also called "static"). Today, nearly everyone on the planet does this. A fixed split means that once the pie is sliced the percentages remain fixed until there is a new negotiation. In spite of the prevalent use of fixed-splits, they *always* create problems of fairness (no exceptions).

You shall soon learn about a new method called a "dynamic" split which allows the ownership percentages to properly adjust without the need for stressful renegotiation. The advantages over a fixed split will be abundantly clear by the time you finish reading this book in a few short, enjoyable hours.

The Minefield

Obviously there are start-ups all over the place who have successfully handled equity allocation issues in their company. Nearly all of them that I've ever heard about slice the pie before or after the value is created. In these cases I can virtually guarantee that at least one of the participants felt mistreated or participants didn't recognize the inequity because they didn't know better

Either way, these are landmines that will eventually explode. The first problem will explode slowly as animosity festers within the organization. The second problem will explode violently when the participants wake up and realize they have been mistreated. Or maybe not...

Maybe the company does so well that they

all choose to focus on the success and be happy with what they did receive. Most successful start-ups get through the early days in spite of their equity allocation problems. They have to, there is no other way.

In my experience, unfortunately, many good ideas do not last because of how the pie is sliced during the nascent stages of the company's existence.

For every company that successfully navigates the minefield, there are a bunch of companies that don't make it because they can't get past the interpersonal problems of equity allocation.

We need a way to prevent problems before they happen.

We Need a Solution

The fundamental problem with using equity as compensation is that equity (pie) has no actual value. It is highly subjective so, lacking a concrete model, entrepreneurs try to assign an actual value. This is virtually impossible at the start-up stage—anything can happen. If actual value is so unclear then what is clear? The answer is *relative* value.

While it's impossible to calculate *actual* value, it is rather simple to calculate *relative* value. We can use relative value to solve the problem.

In order to solve the problem we must find a method for slicing pie that is easy to understand and:

✓ Rewards participants for the relative value of the ingredients they provide
✓ Provides motivation for them to continue to provide more ingredients
✓ Allows founders to fairly add or subtract participants to or from the company
✓ Is flexible in the face of rapid change

Good news. A solution exists. It is called a "Grunt Fund". A Grunt Fund accounts for the relative value of the individual Grunts' inputs so that when it's equity-allocation time it's clear who gets what.

Chapter Two:

The Grunt Fund

Rather than slicing pie before the pie is baked or after the pie is baked and risk creating a herd of disgruntled Grunts, a Grunt Fund allocates equity *while* the pie is being baked by allocating equity based on the relative, theoretical value of the ingredients at any given time. Ta-da!

This provides the basis for the dynamic equity split that I mentioned in the last chapter. Yes, this means that on any given day the pie could be sliced differently. The percentage of pie for each person during the Gap phase remains fluid and changes from day to day. However, to keep things simple, we provide pie instead of actual equity. "Pie" is simply a *promise to allocate actual equity* when the time comes. (You can think of "pie" as an acronym for **P**romise to **I**ssue **E**quity, but you don't have to.)

Some people think this fluidity is strange

and it makes them uncomfortable. When you think through it logically, however, you will see that it makes perfect sense and solves a lot of problems. However, I am aware that it may seem weird at first. After all, it does break conventional wisdom; but, isn't that what being an entrepreneur is all about?

When you use a Grunt Fund you allow Grunts to essentially earn pie over a period of time (during the Gap) based on the theoretical value of the ingredients they provide. So, at any given point in time the allocation among Grunts will vary. This fluidity reflects the ever changing needs of the business as it grows.

To implement a Grunt Fund, follow these simple steps:

1. Appoint a Grunt leader
2. Assign a *theoretical* relative value of the ingredients provided by the various Grunts
3. Calculate the possible equity whenever you need to based on the percentage of value contributed by each Grunt

A Grunt Fund makes some people uneasy. They like to know what they're getting into and they like the I's dotted and T's crossed. That's fine. If this is you then don't use a Grunt Fund-get a job instead.

A job will pay you a fixed salary and you can be around other people like you. Those who can't handle the risk and ambiguity that comes with a start-up are better off in a predictable career with a predictable salary. There's nothing wrong with that. I myself have opted for the job option more than once.

If you are a Grunt, however, you will see that a Grunt Fund is the easiest and most equitable way of slicing the pie.

The Discovery of the Grunt Fund

In his book, The Founder's Dilemmas, Harvard professor Noam Wasserman provides an outline of the perils of bad equity splits and cites the importance of dynamic splits. A reader of an early draft of Slicing Pie brought it to my attention and I was very happy to have found some validation for the concept based on some reliable research. Before I read that book I had never heard of the term "dynamic split" before. Wasserman covers a number of other pitfalls that can sink a start-up so it's high on my list of recommended reads.

A Grunt Fund is a method for creating a dynamic split for your company's equity.

I first discovered pieces of a Grunt Fund when I started a company several years ago on a shoestring budget. I had spent almost a year trying to get the business off the ground. I briefly made the mistake of trying to slice the pie before it was baked when I teamed up with a classmate to enter a business plan competition. My teammate went on to other things after the competition (we won).

Before long, it became clear that I needed help baking the pie and had to find some Grunts. I had no money to pay anyone and I had no idea when I would be able to pay them. So, I made an agreement with each of them that laid the foundation for the Grunt Fund.

I told each Grunt that I was trying to raise money for the business and I was making a case for a $1,000,000 pre-money valuation. I wanted to sell 50% of the company to investors for $1,000,000. I told them to keep track of the hours they spent working at the company and we agreed on an hourly rate for each person.

When I finally raised the money I converted the hours they worked into equity as part of the $1,000,000 valuation. In other words, if an employee worked 100 hours and we agreed to a $100 hourly rate, they would be given equity worth $10,000 of the $1,000,000 or 1%. For the most part, it worked. Everyone got their fair share. It wasn't perfect because I had allocated an unfair percentage to myself, it wasn't intentional, I just didn't know better. (The company lost the funding about a year later so it ultimately didn't matter.)

In all of my experiences, that method worked the best. It was an early building block of a Grunt Fund. Ever since then I've been refining the model so it can adapt to a variety of circumstances. I try to cover all the bases because holes in the model can lead to disagreements among Grunts.

The Grunt Fund Explained

In order to get a better grasp on how a Grunt Fund works, here is a little more detail on the steps and how to calculate the theoretical value.

Step One: Appoint a Leader

All companies need a single leader. Someone has to call the shots. This doesn't mean they don't listen carefully to the other Grunts, it just means they need to step up to the plate and make decisions when no one else will or make the final call on split decisions.

Most of the time picking a leader isn't that hard. Many businesses start because one person got an idea and shared it with others. The person who cares enough about the idea to go out and take action is a good choice. I'll refer to this person as the founder. However, if the founder is smart and knows their shortcomings they may choose to assign leadership to someone with more experience or someone who can dedicate more time to the business in the beginning.

When you pick a leader you will have someone who can manage a Grunt Fund and, if needed, hire or get rid of unproductive Grunts. The Grunt Fund leader is more than someone who simply administers the fund; they are often the person who holds all the equity in the company until it's time to allocate it to others.

Step Two: Assign a theoretical value of the ingredients provided by the various Grunts

Each and every contribution a Grunt can make can be assigned a theoretical value that will allow you to calculate its importance *relative* to other contributions. The Grunt Fund leader will assign these values (with the help of this book) and will keep track of everything. It's not terribly complicated and there are a number of online tools that can make it easier (time and expense tracking software).

By the way, if you've been paying attention, you will notice that I have emphasized the word *theoretical* when it comes to assigning a value to the ingredients provided by the various Grunts. This is important—very important. The contributions that Grunts make have no actual or real value, they only have theoretical value.

If you imply that there is an actual value of the ingredients you may find some of the Grunts want real money- even if you don't have it.

Additionally, if the IRS thinks that your company *actually* has value they might like you to pay some taxes. This is because things can be valued at what people think they are worth. So, if you find a group of people who agree that your company's equity is actually worth something then the IRS would be happy to treat the pie as actual income and assess taxes.

Don't get me wrong, **I'm not recommending that you dodge the IRS.** Nor am I am suggesting that you and your fellow

Grunts just agree that the equity has no value with a wink and a nod. What I am suggesting is that you recognize that reality of your situation is that the **equity has no value**.

This is a jagged little pill for many Grunts and Founder Grunts who like to think that their company is becoming more and more valuable every day. However, until you actually convince someone who has real money to buy into your business the business has no value.

Remember, unless you are using a Grunt-Fund vesting schedule, pie represents a *promise* to allocate a fair share of equity when the time comes. It is not equity and it does not have value. I learned this lesson the hard way…

When I was using the early version of a Grunt Fund in the company I described earlier, I hired a programmer that logged about 160 hours at $50 per hour. He then stopped coming to work. We all wondered what happened to him.

Several weeks later he sent me a bill for $8,000. That's a lot of money for a company that has no money. I had people who had worked for months without expectation of getting paid in cash. I had gone without an income for over a year and invested the bulk of my life savings.

To make matters worse, we couldn't find any evidence that the guy did any real work. It seemed like he was working but he wasn't there long enough to deliver anything. We found a couple of bugs on the bug log with his name on them but that's it.

He wound up pursuing the matter with the Illinois Department of Employment Security. I had to go to arbitration to settle the matter and it was a big hassle. In the end we didn't have to pay, but the lesson was learned.

Make it clear that Grunts, including you, are not creating actual value; you are baking a pie which is based on a theoretical value used for the purposes of calculating a percent ownership. Get it? Good…

Step Three: Calculate the possible equity whenever you need to based on the percentage of value contributed by each Grunt

Whenever anyone wants to know how the pie is sliced they can ask the leader to perform this cute little calculation for each Grunt:

Contribution of Individual Grunt
÷
Total Contributions from All Grunts
=
Individual Grunt's Percent of the Pie

You can do this every day, once a month or whenever you feel like it. This is a rolling pie-slicing plan, meaning that everyone's theoretical ownership will change on a regular basis. This is okay. The people who put in the most work and provide the most value to the organization will have more pie relative to the others.

Remember, slicing pie does not actually grant equity to anyone. For now it is just a way to keep track of what everyone deserves. The pie will show what everyone's possible equity stake *would be* if you actually issued stock to everyone at that particular moment.

In a Grunt Fund, the owner or founder or leader Grunt holds all the equity until it's time to allocate it. In some cases the Grunt Fund may simply determine profit-sharing percentages without using equity at all. I'll talk more about these things later, but just remember that making this work requires a great deal of trust between Grunts. Don't join a Grunt Fund unless you trust the other Grunts.

On that same note, don't form a Grunt Fund unless you are a trustworthy person with a genuine interest in treating people fairly.

Chapter Three:

Creating a Grunt Fund

To create your very own Grunt Fund you simply need to keep track of the relative value of the inputs provided by your herd of Grunts. Each input has its own value. You must agree on how you are going to value the input before it is put into the company (that's what this book is for.)

Determining Value

Ingredients provided have different values. It is essential to have a standard method for determining this value and keep it consistent. If the other Grunts find out that one Grunt is being favored it will appear unfair. Don't worry; incentives for ideas, experience and special talent are built into the methodology.

Consider the following calculations to determine the theoretical value of the ingredients:

Time

Time is pretty much the main contribution of Grunts. It is also the most important contribution. Ideas are nothing without people willing to put the time in to turn it into a company with paying customers.

Determining the value of a person's time, however, can be difficult because people often think they are worth more or less than they actually are. The best way is to determine a realistic *opportunity cost* for their time. Find out what they could earn somewhere else at a similar job (if they could get the job). Getting the number "right" is less important than making sure it's fair *relative* to other Grunts.

Relative value is the key here. Different people are worth different amounts. Clearly, the junior developer straight out of college has a different value than a former SVP of sales for Oracle. So, relatively speaking, the senior guy's time is worth more than the junior guy's time.

However, depending on your company, you may need a junior developer more than you need a hot-shot sales manager. It is up to you to decide who you want to bring on board. Don't make the mistake of taking on more than you need in terms of Grunts, especially high-profile Grunts who may think they are doing you a favor by joining your company. If you choose to slice the pie before or after baking it, it's easy to over-allocate to these kinds of people.

Using a Grunt Fund, the value of an individual's time is based on whatever salary you would have paid them if you had the cash (this is their opportunity cost) *times two*. You double the amount because they are assuming risk by joining an early-stage start-up.

Next, divide the number by 2000 which will help you calculate the Grunt Hourly Resource Rate (GHRR)

I use 2000 hours which is 40 hours per week times 50 weeks per year. This allows for a couple of weeks' vacation and it gives you a nice, round number to work with. Most Grunts work longer than 40 hours per week but it doesn't really matter. What is important is that you keep it consistent from Grunt to Grunt.

Speaking of consistency, it's okay to round the GHRR up to the nearest $10, $50 or $100. If you and your partners had similar earnings levels at your previous jobs you should consider agreeing to the same GHRR for each of you. This isn't a good time to split hairs. Come up with a rate you are comfortable with.

If the job you are hiring a Grunt for is typically paid on an hourly basis, you can simply multiply their hourly rate times two to determine their GHRR.

Make sure the base salaries you use for calculations are realistic. If your company doesn't need a $300,000 CEO then don't hire a $300,000

CEO because their base rate will be too high. Additionally, don't think that just because you're the founder that you should earn the same GHRR as your partner who has 20 years of experience. If I joined a company started by a high school student I would expect to have a higher GHRR. After all, I have lots of experience starting companies plus a college education and two master's degrees. It wouldn't be fair to expect me to take the same rate.

Another rule of thumb is to use a base salary that is commensurate with the job. I may be worth a six-figure salary, but if you hire me to clean the toilets (and I agree) then the base salary should be closer to that of a toilet-cleaner (albeit an experienced toilet cleaner I hope).

So, the theoretical value of a Grunt's time is calculated using their Grunt Hourly Resource Rate or GHRR. The GHRR is the salary you would be willing to pay if you had the cash times two divided by 2000.

All Grunts need to keep track of their hours on a regular basis.

If a Grunt travels for the company you should calculate the travel time as ½ GHRR while in transit.

Time Tracking is a Pain in the Grunt Rump

If the thought of tracking your time makes your skin crawl, you're not alone (I know exactly how you feel). I hate tracking my time. It's a hassle.

That being said, I do it because I know

that it is not only an important way of keeping things fair in a Grunt Fund, but also an invaluable tool for running a start-up.

Start-up companies can be *extremely* time-consuming and time is often the majority of the pie. Knowing how people spend their time is critical because it tells you what people are focused on. You may wonder why you don't have more sales, but if your time records show that 90% of people's time is spent on development projects it will no longer be a mystery. There is no better tool for helping you better manage your staff and set priorities. In business time is money, most businesses keep track of where their money is spent. It only makes sense that they would also track where their time is spent too.

Tracking time brings an important discipline to a start-up that can help keep people focused on the right things and concentrate on productivity. Tools like Harvest make it much easier. I know it can be a hassle, but it becomes routine when you get used to it.

Grunt Daily *Resource Rates*

So many start-up companies have part-time employees and advisors that the hourly rate just makes sense. However, in some cases you may want to use a Grunt *Daily* Resource Rate (GDRR). After you subtract bank holidays, there are 250 business days in a year. So, the calculation for the GDRR is salary times two divided by 250.

This will give you a daily rate to track your time with a typical eight-hour day.

Of course, you may think that you put in a lot more hours per day. This is sometimes true so using the daily rate won't tell the whole story. This is why the hourly rate is more accurate.

The hourly rate is better, but I realize the hassle of tracking every hour can be a burden. If employees are full time the daily rate should work just fine.

Opportunity Cost	Times Risk Premium	GHRR Divide by Hours in a Year	GDRR Divide by Days in a Year
Market Salary	200%	*2000*	*250*
$ 200,000	$ 400,000	$ 200	$ 1,600
$ 175,000	$ 350,000	$ 175	$ 1,400
$ 150,000	$ 300,000	$ 150	$ 1,200
$ 125,000	$ 250,000	$ 125	$ 1,000
$ 100,000	$ 200,000	$ 100	$ 800
$ 75,000	$ 150,000	$ 75	$ 600
$ 50,000	$ 100,000	$ 50	$ 400
$ 25,000	$ 50,000	$ 25	$ 200

A Note about Base Salaries

When you negotiate the base salary that you will use to calculate the GHRR, make sure it is a salary that you would be willing to pay *if* you had the cash. This is important because someday you may want to convert the Grunt to cash compensation and you don't want to pay too much or too little.

In the early days of a start-up founders

either tend to be too generous because they desperately need the help or they tend to be too stingy because they are afraid of the future. To get it right, pretend that you have raised enough money to get your company comfortably past your breakeven point and set salaries that would make sense.

Wages and Grunts

Not all Grunts can afford to forgo salary and may require at least a nominal income to make ends meet. In these cases you should deduct the amount paid to the Grunt from the base salary and use the remainder to calculate the GHRR.

For instance, if a Grunt made $100,000 in their last job their GHRR would be $100,000 x 2 ÷ 2000 which equals $100. If the company paid them a $50,000 salary you would subtract that amount from the base so the new GHRR would be $50,000 x 2 ÷ 2000 which equals $50. In other words, your pie slice is based on whatever compensation is put at risk.

Let me qualify this with a quick note: not all Grunts will earn equity in your business. Sometimes you'll hire a Grunt, pay it a salary and everything is fine and fair. These "mercenary Grunts" are generally more entry-level or with skills that are relatively easy to replace. For instance, a receptionist, a junior web developer, a customer service rep, an entry-level sales rep, unpaid interns and any number of other positions who offer tactical, but probably not strategic, value to the firm. If you can't pay them, however, you will probably have to cut them in.

These people may become pie-seeking Grunts in the future and, although they are still part of the herd, they are happy with money instead of pie as long as you pay them a salary that is commensurate with their experience. If, however, you choose to lower a mercenary Grunt's salary, pay them with pie to make up the difference.

Freelance or Consultant Grunts

If you want to hire a freelance consultant for a well-defined project on a short-term basis then their GHRR is equal to their "start-up" consulting rate *times two*.

Make sure they read a copy of this book so they will understand a Grunt Fund. You should reserve the right to "buy them out" within one year of the last day they render services. You may have to pre-negotiate the buyout rate but never pay more than twice their rate. Remember, you need to compensate them for not only the work they did, but also for the risk they take.

One way to negotiate a buy back with a consultant is to offer them a sliding scale that will build to twice their rate over one year (or two). The scale looks like this for a one-year deal:

Month 1	100%
Month 2	109%
Month 3	118%
Month 4	127%
Month 5	136%
Month 6	145%
Month 7	155%
Month 8	164%
Month 9	173%
Month 10	182%
Month 11	191%
Month 12	200%

So, if you received financing nine months after you stopped working with a contractor you could settle-up with them for 173% of their original bill. This is a pretty nice return for the contractor. A 100% premium might be too high or too low depending on the type of work. As long as you figure it out in advance you should be okay.

After twelve months they receive pie which should translate into an equity grant that they can keep. You can always offer to buy it back after a year, but they should not be required to sell it to you. Remember, they took the risk and helped you when you needed the help. You can't renege later—it's not fair.

The buyback option should have a one-year protection clause that allows the consultant to receive the full value of the shares if the company sells or goes public within 365 days after the buyback occurs.

This will prevent the company from buying back the equity at the last minute before a liquidation event to turn a quick profit at the expense of the Grunt. That would be a dick move (even if it's perfectly legal).

You can use this same method to pay for other sorts of things like supplies, ad space, rent, etc.

An Important Note about Consultants

If the consultant is going to be a long-term member of the team they need to be provided a GHRR that is more in line with what they might earn as a full time employee. A typical consulting rate is much higher than you might pay the same person as an employee. This is because consultants have to charge more to cover the cost of overhead, insurance, marketing, etc.

Let's say I work with a freelance designer who charges me $100 per hour. If he worked for me full time his salary might be more like $50 per hour. I don't mind paying $100 because I don't need a full-time employee.

If I hire the same person for my start-up I would pay him $200 as a freelance Grunt or $100 as a regular Grunt. If the person is going to be an ongoing member of the team the regular Grunt rate should apply. An ongoing member of the team would eventually work for the company full time if the company grows.

The key here is to make sure the rate you pay is fair to the other Grunts working just as hard. Just because one person has done freelance work it doesn't mean they should be paid higher than everyone else.

Generally speaking, a freelance or consultant Grunt would do one or two small projects that have fairly discrete deliverables. If a person is part of the team, making decisions with the team, and helping to shape the direction of the company they are not freelance or consultant Grunts. They are regular Grunts or part-time Grunts and should be treated like a member of the herd.

Milestones

Unfortunately, earning pie with hours does provide incentive to work more hours, which is something you will want to keep an eye on. In some cases, you may want to provide extra encouragement for getting something done and extra *dis*couragement for taking too much time.

You can do this by sitting with the herd and discussing how much time it will take to reach important milestones. For instance, your developer may estimate 80 hours to complete a working prototype. The hours will be accrued only when and if the milestone is met and only up to the agreed-upon hours.

There are a couple of things to keep in mind when doing this to avoid conflict. First, you must resist the temptation to change the timing and the scope of milestones. If you do, you may have to accept the hours spent working towards a changed milestone even if it's not met. It's impossible to know, in advance, what activities and behaviors will be most important or what will change. You can't penalize a Grunt for acting in good faith.

Second, if the project moves faster your developer will still have incentive to take the extra hours. In this example you will be allowing 80 hours for a job that may have otherwise taken 40.

If you see people gaming the system you may have to have a little Grunt-to-Grunt talk with them.

Grunts on Boards

While most start-up companies don't have formal boards of directors until formal money comes in, it is not uncommon for a start-up to form a board of advisors. These are often unpaid professionals with domain expertise who volunteer to help a start-up get off the ground by offering advice, guidance, important introductions and other inputs that not only help the company get started, but also add credibility to the concept which is comforting for potential investors.

The involvement of these people can vary dramatically and they usually don't expect to be paid, but giving them pie is fair if they are providing real value. A Grunt Fund can accommodate these people quite nicely as long as their GHRR isn't unreasonable. Because advisors are often successful people, they can command high salaries and, therefore, high hourly rates. These rates can get out of control pretty quick for the average start-up.

One way to manage this is to develop an "advisory plan" that sets a fixed rate for an advisory board member's time and a minimum number of hours before a slice of the pie is cut for them.

For instance, you could tell them that, as a member of the advisory board, they are entitled to a $200 GHRR starting after ten dedicated hours. So, when they hit ten hours they would get a slice equal to $2,000 of the TBV (Theoretical Base Value—more on this later) and they would begin participating as a Grunt. Unlike a consultant Grunt, a buyout option probably doesn't make sense given that the money may not be significant and their ongoing relationship with the firm would be beneficial.

Maximum GHRR

In general, I recommend capping the maximum GHRR at $200 to keep things from getting too skewed. This rate implies that a person's opportunity cost is over $200,000 a year. The typical Grunt would not fall into this range (80% of Americans make under $100,000).

It may not be uncommon for a more experienced entrepreneur or business advisor to have a high earning potential, but GHRRs of over $200 tend to be de-motivating for other Grunts. If someone wants much higher rates than that then early-stage start-ups may not be the best choice.

Pie A La Mode

Advisory Board Member Letter
To see a sample offer letter used to invite an Advisor to a Grunt Fund company, visit **SlicingPie.com** and click Pie à la Mode or scan the code.

Absentee Owners

Most of the time, a buyout right is important when dealing with people who are not employees. Anyone who owns equity or options in your business who is not an investor or an employee is known as an "absentee owner" (Also known as "Dead Equity"). Prospective investors will be wary of a business that has too many absentee owners.

Absentee owners can be difficult to manage and may have rights and make demands that can distract the business. The ideal number of absentee owners is zero. However, if you are in the Gap and have no cash, then allowing absentee owners may be your only option. The right investor will respect that kind of tenacity but they will still appreciate being able to buy out the absentee owners. In other words, they can "cash-out" the individual.

Cash

People are much more likely to provide ingredients like equipment or time than money so an extra incentive is preferable for those who provide cold, hard cashola.

If a Grunt provides small amounts of working capital, pays for services (like corporate formation), or covers material out-of-pocket expenses for which no reimbursement will be received, the theoretical value is the value of the cash or credit used *times four*.

Cash contributions are weighted heavily in a formation-stage company for several reasons. First, it is much harder for a Grunt to replace the cash when he or she is in the process of starting a company. Unless they have money to spare (and most Grunts don't), the Grunt must either keep a day job or find consulting work to pay the bills in the short term. Starting a business and trying to earn a living at the same time takes a lot more energy than doing one or the other.

Next, all businesses need cash to survive.

No cash = No business

Grunts like pie and if they can buy a big slice for putting in a little cash, everybody wins.

Lastly, weighting cash heavily allows founders to buy and maintain a big chunk of their own business during the early days.

Many founders want to retain ownership of their company and tend to be stingy about slicing pie. The best way to retain equity is to simply pay in cash. If you don't have the cash you can use equity, but you can't expect to keep most of the pie yourself.

Put this in perspective. If you simply *pay* people for the contribution they provide you can keep all the pie for yourself. However, if you want to start something from nothing, you are going to have to share it.

To recap, the theoretical value of a cash or cash-equivalent contribution a Grunt makes is the amount of the contribution *times four*.

The Well

The cash rule causes some people angst. They figure at 4x someone can plunk a big chunk of cash in the company and own the lion's share of the equity. This is true and may be fine if the cash is used to pay people their fair market rate. However, if the cash isn't used to pay people the unpaid people may feel demotivated. It's important that the allocation of equity fairly reflects the risk that individuals take when they make contributions to the company.

Cash sitting in a bank account is not really at risk because unused cash can be returned to the owner. In a traditional investment the company takes the cash in exchange for a fixed amount of equity. The incentive is to spend the money because the equity is already granted. In a Grunt Fund we want to encourage people to only use what they actually need. The concept of the Well can help.

Cash can be taken into the company as a loan to create a "Well" of money that can be drawn from as needed. Only when the money is spent will it be converted to pie. This aligns the incentives of the investor (who wants to reduce risk) and the Grunt (who wants to be smart about how they spend. With a Well, Grunts can take sips of cash when needed.

Sometimes Grunts only need sips of cash

A Note about Cash Investments from Grunts Who Also Get Wages

A Grunt that receives current cash compensation should not be allowed to simply re-invest the cash in an effort to get pie at a higher rate.

For example let's say my market rate is

$50 per hour which would translate into a GHRR of $100. Instead of pie, the company pays me my market rate (if they have the money), so I do not get pie for the time I put into the company. If, however, I put the money they paid me back into the company I would get the 4 x rate. So, instead of getting $100 in pie (which is what I would have received for my time) I would get $200 at the cash rate. That's not fair.

Generally speaking, a Grunt that receives wages is one that does not have the money to invest. However, if they *really* want to invest, the 4 x rate should only apply to cash investment in excess of what they were paid. Any money they invest that is less than what they have been paid should go in at the 2 x rate.

A Note about Crowd-Funded Cash

As of this writing, the impact of the JOBS Act is still up in the air. Theoretically, it will lower the restrictions on the sale of equity to non-accredited investors.

The problem with allocating small slices of pie to complete strangers is that you wind up with a bunch of absentee owners that could turn into a *major* administrative headache.

It is for this reason that cash from crowd-funding sites is *less valuable to you*. So, while cash from people on the team or close to the business might get a 4x value in pie, you might want to give the crowd-funded cash 2x or 1x. You will still be giving pie to random people, but at least you won't be giving them as much. This is fair because of the additional complexity that comes with managing shareholders.

A Note for Grunt Leaders

It's the job of the leader to make sure everyone is playing fairly and getting what they deserve. Overt trickery (like reinvesting wages in order to get the higher rate in pie) should not be allowed.

A Grunt who habitually tries to "work the system" clearly does not understand the intended spirit of teamwork and may need to be removed from the herd (more later on this).

To combat against other tricks, the leader should not accept cash investments that are significantly more than the company actually needs at any given time, this will help manage the pie better and prevent abuse.

Loans and Credit

Sometimes a Grunt will personally guarantee a loan or use their own credit cards for the company. If the Grunt pays the bill, the money he or she uses to pay it should be treated like cash—the amount of money *times four*.

However, if the company pays the bill the Grunt will receive *no pie* as long as the bill is paid on time.

The company should always cover interest charges and, if the company does no pay the bill on time, the company should cover late charges.

However, if the company *can't* pay it off at all, the Grunt who provided the credit *must* pay it off by him or herself. In these cases, the payments are treated as cash contributions.

So, the theoretical value of loans and credit provided with a personal guarantee is *nothing* if the company makes the payments. If the Grunt makes the payments the amount of the payments is treated as a cash investment so it's the amount of the payment *times four.*

Big Loans

The above loan rules apply no matter how large the loan.

"Major" loans, like Small Business Administration (SBA) loans or mortgages on real estate (like for a rental property), get treated like any other loans. *No pie* is given for the loan if the payments are covered by the operations of the business.

Example One:

Joe and Frank buy a rental property for $100,000. Frank secures the mortgage with his assets, but he splits the $20,000 down payment and closing costs with Joe— $10,000 each. The mortgage payment is paid from the proceeds of the rental income.

Both Joe and Frank receive pie for their cash ($40,000 each), but Frank gets nothing for securing the loan. That's it.

If the owners have to pony up more money because the house isn't rented they will receive pie according to the cash rules.

The value of the house has nothing to do with the theoretical value of the business. Only the cash inputs count.

Example Two:

Kendra and Millie buy a scarf company from Robin for $100,000. Using their personal assets as collateral, they secure an $80,000 SBA loan.

Kendra fronts the $20,000 to complete the purchase, plus an additional $20,000 to cover operating expenses and some new marketing efforts for the company. Millie puts in no cash.

The cash from Kendra goes into the theoretical value according to the cash rule (times four). So, Kendra's input gets her $40,000 x 4 or $160,000. Note that this exceeds the actual value of the company. This is still fair, Kendra has taken on some serious risk. The actual value of the company ($100,000) has no bearing on the Grunt Fund.

This May Sound Strange

There are at least two things about dealing with loans that might seem strange at first:

1. Disregarding the actual value of something

purchased with a loan
2. Disregarding the security behind the loan

The Grunt Fund disregards the value of the underlying asset because Grunt Funds deal with the *inputs* from the different Grunts to create a theoretical value, not an actual value. So, actual value doesn't really matter much.

Let's pretend, for a minute, that actual value *does* matter. In that case we would account for the actual value of the asset, but, because there is an outstanding loan, the liability would offset the actual value so it's a wash.

As for providing pie to whoever secures the loan, the Grunt Fund ignores this because there is no practical way to translate this into pie. It's too subjective.

One could argue that the person who secures the loan should be rewarded because it's their butt on the line if things fall apart. That is a valid point. However, with no objective way to value the risk we have to ignore it.

With Grunt Funds we only count what we can count. If we can't count it, we don't count it. Don't lose too much sleep over this; it all works out in the end.

If a Grunt doesn't like this they can opt not to secure the loan — even if it means an end to the business. Nobody has to take risks if it makes them uncomfortable.

Putting actual cash in the business is always the fastest way to earn pie. If you feel like you deserve more pie, put in more cash.

Loans from a Grunt to the Company

When a Grunt loans money to the company the Grunt is entitled to the same thing any other lender is entitled to which is repayment of principal and interest. The interest rate should be set to whatever the Grunt is willing to accept. No pie will be given if the company is paying as agreed.

If the company defaults on the loan, the balance of the loan can be treated like a cash contribution according to the cash rule.

Supplies and Equipment

Although supplies and equipment are important ways to offset cash expenses, their cash-value is often difficult to assess. If the supplies and resources *facilitate* the business, meaning they help make running the business easier (pens, paper, temporary office space, personal computers, etc) their value may be incidental to the theoretical value of the business and should not be taken into account at all. Despite the expense incurred by the individual participant, the act of accounting for such inputs may cause more damage to the relationship than it is worth at an early stage.

Think about it. If a Grunt shows up with a box of pencils should they really expect to receive pie in exchange?

A potential investor will likely place little

or no value on access to personal computers or office supplies. Such expenses should be ignored during the early days of a fledgling business.

Eventually these expenses could be covered by the business. However, it is rarely advisable to reimburse past expenses from an early-stage investment fund. The expenses are sunk and offer no future value to the company. Investors loathe using their investment dollars to pay off debt and will pass on deals that have too much.

Old laptops and pencils are one thing, but if a Grunt is going to the office supply store on a weekly basis and spending hundreds of dollars on supplies that's a different thing. In those cases the purchase of supplies should be treated as an expense for which reimbursement is not expected which is equivalent to cash. **Note to Grunts**: save your receipts!!!

In some cases, equipment and supplies *enable* the business. Without them the business would not exist, so having access to them is material to the value of the business and would be valued by potential early-stage investors. For instance, if you are starting a t-shirt printing company a screen-printing press would be a piece of business enabling equipment.

If the Grunt acquired the asset specifically for the business then it should be treated as an out-of-pocket expense for which no reimbursement is expected (cash).

If, before joining the herd, the Grunt owned the asset for less than a year it should be valued at the price the Grunt paid. For instance, the Grunt may have a few servers leftover from a previous business that are less than a year old and still in good shape.

    If the supplies or equipment are older than a year the value should be set to the same amount as it would have cost the company to acquire the asset from a third party. If it's a car, for instance, you could use the value listed in the Kelly Blue Book or take it to Car Max to see what they might give you.

    The value of most items can be assessed with a quick glance at other items selling on Ebay. Ebay sets the standard for what people are willing to pay for just about anything.

    It's okay to err on the side of generosity because the Grunt providing the asset is assuming the risk that they may not get it back.

    To summarize, calculate the contribution of supplies and equipment as follows:

✓ Zero if the contribution simply *facilitates* the business

If the contribution *enables* the business:

✓ Treat as a cash equivalent if it was acquired specifically for the business
✓ Use the purchase value if it is less than a year old
✓ Use the resale value if it is more than a year old

Grunts who contribute business-enabling supplies and equipment for which they do not receive payment can be compensated fairly with pie.

Facilities

Office space, warehouse space, retail space and other facilities that enable the business have value, especially when the Grunt could otherwise rent or lease it to a paying customer.

If the facility is appropriate for the business it is fair to value the facility equal to the amount the Grunt could otherwise lease or rent the space (not as cash). An appropriate facility is one that the business might rent or lease in order to run the business if they had the cash.

Sometimes the facility will work, even though it's not ideal. For instance, if you need small office space and a Grunt in your herd offers use of an entire floor in one of his or her buildings you probably have access to more than you need. In such cases your fledging company shouldn't be expected to provide pie to cover the entire value. The fair value is proportionate to what the business needs in order to grow and prosper.

Also, space in someone's house probably shouldn't be exchanged for pie unless the person would otherwise rent the space to a different business. People don't usually rent their garages to start-up companies.

I once started a company and was able to negotiate some office space from a friend of mine who owned a marketing agency. My team and I took over a few cubes in the corner of the office. It worked out nicely. We only paid for the space we used and had free Internet access and use of the phones for a nominal price. This is ideal. Ask around, situations like this are sometimes easy to come by.

Ideas and Intellectual Property

There are two ways to reward Grunts for business-enabling ideas and related Intellectual property: The first is to calculate the theoretical value of the idea and the second is to provide an ongoing royalty payment (cash or pie) to the inventor. You can use both, if appropriate.

It's important to remember that ideas without action are relatively valueless, no matter how good the idea is. In the start-up world, a dozen ideas are worth about a dime, less the cost of the lunch over which the ideas were generated. Generally, ideas should *not* be taken into account in a Grunt Fund *unless* they fit the following criteria:

1. The idea must have existed before the inception of the business
2. The idea must be original
3. The idea must be non-obvious
4. The idea must be "baked" as opposed to

"half-baked".

Selling Halloween costumes in October is obvious and unoriginal. Therefore, it should receive no pie.

That doesn't mean you can't make plenty of money with an idea that is as unoriginal and obvious as selling Halloween costumes. Sometimes better execution is all it takes. You could make millions if you have the right people.

In the case of unoriginal and obvious ideas it's the execution that really counts. Most businesses today are founded on unoriginal and obvious ideas. This is good, these ideas could have a huge market and you won't have to reinvent the wheel.

A book about implementing a dynamic equity split, however, is both original (there are no others like it) and not obvious. It may be obvious in hindsight, but most entrepreneurs are unaware of the concept until it is brought to their attention (otherwise everybody would be using dynamic splits). This doesn't mean that nobody has ever used a dynamic equity split before, but the details presented in this book are not widely known (yet).

A "baked" idea often comes in the form of a polished concept, a thoughtful business model or legal protection. They require insight, experience and creativity. Baked ideas usually represent the investment of considerable time and money and are often business enablers. This book, for example, is baked.

Ideas that fit the above criteria have value that should be taken into account. Ideas developed during the regular course of business, however, would not be taken into account no matter how good the idea is. It's the nature of business to generate new, good ideas and it is part of the job of a Grunt to come up with the most awe-inspiring new idea that ever existed.

Calculating the value of ideas and intellectual property can be a challenge because inventors tend to really overestimate the value of their ideas. People tend to say things like, "Michael Dell stole my idea for building computers in my dorm room! That crook made billions! He owes me." It's ridiculous.

Don't get me wrong, ideas are critical to a business' success. But turning the idea into a reality is usually where the value is built, not in coming up with the idea in the first place. This doesn't mean you can't give someone who came up with a great idea some pie as a bonus. But be careful not to put too much emphasis on the idea itself. Ideas, even good ideas, are plentiful. It's the initiative, passion, action and grit that turn ideas into good businesses.

If the idea is well documented and baked the value is set equal to the amount of time it took to bake the idea times the originator's GHRR plus the costs of any research or legal protection.

So, if I spend 500 hours developing a business plan around my idea, 200 hours writing and researching a patent and $10,000 hiring a lawyer to file my patent then the idea would be worth 700 x my GHRR plus $10,000 ($80,000).

GHRR	**$100/hour**
Business plan hours	500 hours
Patent research hours	200 hours
Time @ GHRR	$70,000
Legal fees	$10,000
Theoretical Value of the IP	***$80,000***

Royalties

In addition to calculating the theoretical value of the intellectual property, it may be appropriate to also provide a royalty payment to the inventor. Royalties reflect the fact that without the idea the business would not be possible and that the idea itself is generating buzz or recognition for the company. Additionally, royalties *only* reward ideas that actually help the company generate revenues.

I recently spoke to a guy, we'll call him "Ted", who wanted to start a Grunt Fund with another guy who we'll call "Xerxes", who had been working on a technology product for six months. Ted thought that Xerxes would have been better off building a more basic product to test the concept instead of the robust prototype that was actually built. Ted was concerned that the theoretical value of the idea and related work was going to be too high. If Ted and Xerxes had been working together since day one, Ted could have helped Xerxes design a more basic product for testing. In this case Ted could offer a royalty to Xerxes that would only provide pie when the product actually generates revenue. This way if the product turns out to be a dud, Ted won't feel that Xerxes has too much pie. Likewise, if the idea turns out to be a winner, Xerxes will be properly rewarded.

Solo entrepreneurs who spend years developing their ideas often over value their time. Royalties can help address time invested before the team actually forms.

Royalty payments are generally paid based on a percent of revenue or cash receipts. Paying a royalty based on profits is not recommended because profits can be manipulated at the inventor's expense.

The percent you actually pay will vary based on the industry standards and your negotiating skills. Be sure to negotiate a fair rate because you may someday be paying out in cash.

Royalties are kind of like commissions (see below). You can either choose to pay all or part of the royalty in cash or give them a slice of pie equal to *two times* the unpaid royalty.

You can ask for a buyback provision for the pie, but it is okay to issue stock to the inventor when the time comes because investors will see the inventor's interests aligned with the business and won't consider it "dead equity". It

can be a good idea to stay close to the inventor
unless they are one of those mad-scientist types
that spend their free time trying to acquire human
brains to control robots and household
appliances.

Lastly, in some cases it is appropriate to
cap or "expire" the royalty payments. This is
important because a perpetual royalty may turn
off potential investors. (Investors don't like deals
they can't get out of.)

Traditional licensing deals often include an
advanced payment against royalties. This prevents
companies from securing rights to intellectual
property they don't plan on monetizing. I don't
recommend pie advances because it doesn't jive
well with the spirit of the Grunt Fund.

Relationships

The last input that requires discussion is
relationships. Sometimes Grunts provide access
to certain people that the company needs, but
might not know. The right relationships can turn
into sales or partnerships, a professional service
provider, a reliable vendor or an investor. A well-
connected Grunt can do wonders for a company
and that value should be taken into account.

However, be careful not to be too bullish
about the prospect of a Grunt's relationships
actually materializing as relationships with the
company. I've been in more than one situation
where a start-up has over-paid for an employee
based on the quality of their relationships. Once

they were on board, the relationships failed to turn into anything substantial. In many cases even if the relationship does materialize it is difficult to quantify the value in any meaningful way.

Relationships are kind of like intellectual property, the relationship has low value unless you put the time and effort into making it work. However, a notable exception is a relationship that turns into a sale.

Nothing is more important in the early days of a start-up's life than an actual customer that pays its bills.

A business needs customers and, as obvious as it sounds, many start-up companies don't have customers. They're too busy building products, designing slick web sites, writing ads, creating business plans, negotiating legal contracts and talking to each other.

The best way to translate relationships into value is simply by applying the GHRR to the hours spent cultivating the relationship after the Grunt joins the herd. If the relationship has the potential to turn into a sale, you should set up a commission structure or bonus for the Grunt that would reward them for successfully landing the sale. The Grunt should receive a theoretical value of twice the unpaid commission they might otherwise earn if they were getting cash.

For instance, if you agree to pay a 5% commission the theoretical value would be 10%. If you paid out 2.5% in cash the theoretical value of the unpaid commission would be 5%.

So, at a 5% rate if the sales person had a connection that resulted in a $20,000 sale the 5% commission would be $1,000. You could give them $2,000 in pie, or if you paid them $500 of the commission in cash, you would give them $1,000 in pie because only $500 of the $1,000 would be at risk.

Similarly, if a Grunt's relationship provides a significant Series A investment, a finder's fee might be appropriate. A typical finder's fee is 5% on the first million and 2.5% on funds over a million. The finder's fee would convert to equity at the same terms the investor receives (not Grunt-Fund terms).

Other Resources/Partnerships

If a Grunt or business partner can provide temporary access to important resources they should receive pie in exchange for at least part of the opportunity costs of letting the company use the asset. For instance, a Grunt may have a forklift for another company that your company could rent from time to time. In these cases you should negotiate a reasonable rate in pie. If the asset would otherwise be rented to another client the rate could be set to the rental rate times two to account for the risk. If the asset would not otherwise be rented then a fair rate can be negotiated.

The same would apply to certain human resources. For example, my company, (Lake Shark Ventures, LLC) employees a number of people who work on company projects. When I make investments into start-up companies I often invest the resources of my company at a very reasonable rate in pie. They aren't freelancers, nor are they employees of the company, nor are they unreimbursed expenses. They are Lake Shark employees that work on projects for start-up companies. I pay them out of my own pocket. Lake Shark takes pie.

This scenario can be quite common and can form the basis for important partnerships and alliances that your company needs. Most of the time there is no set rule; you would simply negotiate a GHRR that makes sense for the company and for the partner.

Vacations

During the early days of a start-up company things are so fluid that a formal vacation policy doesn't make much sense. Grunts should not get pie when they are on vacation. (Unless they are working on vacation in which case they would receive pie for the time they work).

Grunt Funds account for actions and behaviors that contribute to the building of a company. Sitting on a beach sipping piña coladas doesn't help a new company much so pie is not provided.

Later on, when the company is more mature, you can create a more formalized vacation policy. My favorite is one with no cap on vacation days provided the employee is doing their job and meeting goals and expectations. This allows employees to manage their own time and sends the message that managers respect their ability to behave like adults with a sense of responsibility. It's also easier to manage because you don't have to pay people for unused vacation days or split hairs about what constitutes a vacation day, sick day, or personal day.

This has nothing to do with the Grunt Fund, but like a Grunt Fund it is based on mutual trust and respect. Now…back to the model.

Summary Calculations

The following table summarizes the theoretical value of the various ingredients:

Ingredient	Calculation
Time- Grunt	Grunt Hourly Resource Rate (GHRR)= negotiated base annual salary x 2 ÷ 2000 (or 250 for a Grunt *Daily* Resource Rate- GDRR)
Time- Grunt who also gets cash compensation	GHRR = (negotiated base annual salary – current compensation) x 2 ÷ 2000
Time- Consultant	Hourly rate x 2 (reserve the right to buy back)
Money- Cash	Amount of money x 4 (2x if crowd-funded)
Money- Personal credit, paid off by Company	Nadda
Money- Personal credit, paid off by Grunt	Amount of money paid towards bill (including interest) x 4
Money- Loan to the company	No pie, just principle and interest from the company. Treat as cash if not repaid by company.
Money- Unreimbursed expenses	Amount of expenses x 4

Ingredient	Calculation
Supplies and equipment- business *facilitating*	Nothing
Supplies and equipment- business *enabling*	✓ Treat as a *cash equivalent* if it was acquired specifically for the business ✓ Use the *purchase value* if it is less than a year old ✓ Use the *resale* value if it is more than a year old
Facilities	✓ Equal to rent or lease amount if appropriate for business ✓ Equal to cost of more appropriate facility
Ideas & intellectual property	✓ Development hours times GHRR plus costs ✓ Unpaid royalty x 2
Relationships	Unpaid commission x 2 or finder's fee for investment
Other resources	Negotiated rate

If you don't like these calculations you can make up your own. Just keep it fair and consistent.

Pie A La Mode

Cheat Sheet
To download a cheat sheet with summary calculations visit **SlicingPie.com** and click Pie à la Mode or scan the code.

Put it all together and bake for 12-18 months. Delicious! Pies that take too long to bake get kind of boring…

Chapter Four:

Using a Grunt Fund

Now that you have determined the value of the various ingredients in the pie you have a simple way of calculating everyone's share. You simply add up the theoretical value of the ingredients contributed by a single Grunt and divide by the total theoretical value of the ingredients contributed by *all* the Grunts. This will give you the percent contribution of a single Grunt that you can convert to equity whenever you want.

Contribution of Individual Grunt
÷
Total Contributions from All Grunts
=
Individual Grunt's Percent of the Pie

The   total   theoretical   value   of   all   the

contributions is called the Theoretical Base Value (TBV). To determine ownership percentages divide the theoretical value of each Grunt's input by the TBV.

Individual Grunts should keep track of the hours they spend on the business and how they spent the hours. Keep enough detail so that it's meaningful, but not so much that it is aggravating. Keeping the balance is up to you. I once worked for a man who tracked his time in 15-minute increments—probably an overkill for the average Grunt. Still, it is nice to know how Grunts spend their time in a start-up business.

A simple time sheet could look a little like this:

Date	Hours	Notes
1/5	9.50	Worked on business plan, lunch with potential client, interviewed printing vendors
1/6	8.25	Discussed plan with Frank, prepared investor presentation, met with Joe about web site, reviewed and edited specs
1/7	4.50	Edited web site specs
1/8	1.75	Stared out the window

Grunts should also keep track of the other ingredients they provide and submit them regularly to the founder or lead Grunt. You can use whatever format you are comfortable with, but make sure you keep track of the different inputs.

When to Calculate Equity

For the most part, you will want to calculate it on a regular basis, say monthly, to see where everyone stands. More importantly, however, you will want to calculate it if you anticipate that someone, like a potential investor, will ask about it.

I started a business a few years ago where I wound up pitching the business dozens of times to potential investors. If I was using a Grunt Fund, I would have needed to have the equity allocation numbers handy just in case I needed them. Investors often want to know about ownership.

In some cases (such as small investors) you can tell them the current equity allocation, but explain to them that you are using this system and let them buy their own copy of the book. It will be good for them to know how you are calculating it and they will think you are a fair and wise person. It will also help me sell more copies so it's a win for you and for me.

Order a Six-Pack of Slicing Pie
To get a special price on six copies of Slicing Pie for your team visit **SlicingPie.com/sixers** or scan the code.

However, when real investment dollars come in they may not be subject to the cash rule (4x) how much of the pie will depend on your ability to negotiate and set a good pre-money valuation. Significant outside investors, in other words, may not be Grunts.

Calibration

In a perfect world the value of equity would go up in excess of the theoretical value of the various inputs.

This is the point of a growth-oriented business. Often, when you pitch a potential investor you are trying to sell them on a base value that is hopefully more than you and the other Grunts have put into the business. Successfully negotiating a high valuation is very motivating for Grunts and it breathes more life into the business.

However, you can set a new TBV earlier in a start-up's life with a slightly different purpose: adding Grunts to the herd.

Sometimes, if you and other Grunts have worked hard on the company for a period of time, you may want to "harvest" a little of the value for yourselves before allowing others into the herd. This is fair, early Grunts take on more risk than later Grunts. I call this "Calibration".

Pretend that you and two other Grunts have each put in $30,000 worth of theoretical value into a company. You have been working for six months and you need to bring on more people. The company has a little traction now so you would like to reap some of the benefits for your hard work. You allocate the equity at 33% each on a TBV of $90,000. If you think the company is now "worth" $300,000 you can move the base to $300,000 and move forward as if you had all contributed $100,000 each. On paper your investment of time and whatever else you put in has grown threefold.

Now, when other Grunts enter the herd they will be earning against a base of $300,000 instead of $90,000. So, if they contributed $100,000 in value and the rest of you did nothing, they would have earned 25% of the company ($100,000/$400,000) instead of over 50% of the company ($100,000/$90,000). This allows early Grunts to keep a higher percent for themselves. Keep in mind, however, that the new work the original Grunts contribute will be calculated against this new TBV so they will consume pie at a slower rate.

The other thing to keep in mind is that if you calibrate too high you run the risk of exceeding the value you can sell to an investor, which would mean that when you do find an investor, newer Grunts will actually realize less value than they feel they contributed which is a good way to anger a good Grunt. I could tell myself and the other Grunts that the company is worth $1 billion, but if I can only convince an investor it's worth $1 million I will have disappointed my Grunts.

It's best to calibrate only when enough value has been built that an early herd deserves to benefit from the higher-risk work.

Also, as time goes by, a Grunt Fund will have to be replaced with a different method of allocation. As a company grows it may take on a more formal structure to handle equity sharing.

Pie Partitioning

As an alternative to calibration (which some people find confusing) you can simply create a "partition" in your pie which isolates a hunk for you and your fellow super-early-stage founders. The partitioned part will maintain its percentage no matter what. For instance, you could partition off 10% of the pie and use the Grunt Fund to divvy up the rest. The 10% will always be worth 10%. So, the other Grunts will earn a percent of what's left over (the 90%).

No matter what you do you are all eventually going to run into a situation where you have percentages of percentages and it will get harder to get your head around it. This is sort of unavoidable so brace yourself!

Outgrowing the Grunt Fund

When your company gets big enough you will outgrow your Grunt Fund. Mostly because your incremental percentage of pie gets smaller as time goes by. In the beginning your 10 hours of work may be equal to 50% of the company if your partner also works 10 hours. Later, when the company has a $500,000 TBV your 10 hours won't get you very much. By this time you are probably ready to start looking for real investors. When you get the cash you can hire a lawyer and an accountant to put together a nice option program.

When you sit down with your lawyer you can tell them exactly how many shares each person on the team should receive. Remember, the TBV has *no bearing* on the value of your company. It simply provided a means to calculate percentages.

Chapter Five:

Subtracting a Grunt

Few events take their toll on a start-up company more than when a Grunt leaves. It is highly disruptive. Sometimes they are no longer interested in the project or no longer share the vision. Other times they have other obligations, such as family, that forces them back into day jobs and sometimes the Grunt isn't a good fit with the herd and has to be asked to leave.

When a Grunt leaves the herd, either by choice or by force, great care must be taken to treat the Grunt fairly. Even if the Grunt is being fired for being a total jerk there is still proper and fair treatment. If, as the herd's leader, you treat a departing Grunt unfairly, you will do damage to the entire herd. The last thing you want is a herd of disgruntled Grunts.

Besides treating a Grunt with dignity and respect, fair treatment includes how much pie a departing Grunt is or is not entitled to as well as what the company is entitled to in terms of pie buy-back or non-competition. When a Grunt leaves and keeps his or her pie they will become an absentee owner which, as mentioned before, is something to avoid if possible and fair.

Determining who is entitled to what will depend largely on the circumstances of their departure. There are three main reasons a Grunt will leave the herd:

- ✓ They might resign
- ✓ They might be fired
- ✓ They may no longer be able to work because they become disabled or dead

Resignation

When a Grunt resigns, or quits, the motivation to do so falls into two buckets. The first bucket is called "resignation without cause" the second is called "resignation with good cause".

Resignation Without Cause

Sometimes a Grunt loses interest in the company or sometimes they have external pressures that prevent them from being able to contribute to the company in a meaningful way.

So, the Grunt resigns. In the case of resignation without cause, the Grunt has broken its commitment to the company and should not expect to retain the same slice of the pie as they would have as an employee. It's a free country and there is no reason why a Grunt can't move on to what they feel are greener pastures. But, you can't have your pie and eat it too!

When a Grunt resigns without cause, they will forfeit *all* of the pie earned in the Grunt Fund through the *time* they contributed to the company.

Next, the company should recalculate the theoretical value of the Grunt's other contributions *without* the multipliers. The new theoretical value becomes the value of what the company would have paid for supplies and equipment (if they could have) and the actual value of the cash.

This may sound a little harsh, but by agreeing in advance to reduce the theoretical value of a Grunt's inputs, you are creating an incentive not to leave. Retaining employees is important and a Grunt Fund has this built-in retention program.

Additionally, the company should reserve the right to buy back the pie at a price equal to the new theoretical value.

If possible, pay back any cash contributions the Grunt has made especially if the Grunt is leaving for financial reasons. You may want the Grunt back for a future herd—treat all Grunts fairly.

Leaving the herd in the lurch has consequences and it should. When a Grunt resigns and maintains its original slice of pie, the

Company will have lost a piece of itself that they may need in order to provide incentive to a replacement Grunt.

In the movie Startup.com, the president of a dot-com company has to negotiate a buyout of the stock owned by an early partner who had left the company. He wound up paying $800,000. Ouch. This was money that could have been put to better use than paying off a former employee who left on a whim! This guy, as it turns out, was pretty much the only guy who made any money off their stock!

The other issue is non-competition. In the case of resignation without cause the company should secure a non-compete agreement in exchange for letting the Grunt keep the pie in the company. This will provide a deterrent to Grunts who want to take what they learned with you and start a competing business. Many states won't support a non-compete, but some will. Make sure you have been clear that the Grunt was never promised any cash from the business.

Even if you live in a state that won't enforce the non-compete agreement ask them to sign it anyway. Just like the Grunt Fund is a moral contract, so is the non-compete. Sure, the Grunt can break his or her promise, but if they are a good person they should recognize that they were treated fairly. They should treat you fairly as well.

By the way, the leaving Grunt does not get their stuff back if they brought anything. When a Grunt provides supplies and equipment it generally becomes property of the company. The same goes for ideas and intellectual property. If the Grunt holds a patent to the idea in their name they should have already given the company an exclusive right to the idea. In most cases, even if they are fired, Grunts entitled to royalty payments will continue to receive them at the Grunt Fund rate (unpaid royalty x 2).

Sometimes a Grunt loses interest in the company

When a Grunt leaves a company because they can't afford to work with no income, and the company can't afford to pay them, it may be appropriate to keep the Grunt as a part-time member of the herd and allow them to keep their pie. Don't play hardball with Grunts if you don't have to.

Resignation With Good Cause

Sometimes a Grunt is "pushed-out" of a company or compelled to leave because the other Grunts made decisions that changed the situation so much for the Grunt that it's not what they originally signed up for.

In some cases the decisions are unavoidable, in other cases the decision seemed more important than the negative impact it would have on the affected Grunt. Such decisions would include:

✓ *Adverse change in title or responsibilities.* If the Vice Grunt of Marketing was demoted to the Director of Operations, the Grunt would have a good cause to leave. They wouldn't have to leave, but the role is clearly no longer what they signed up for.

✓ *Adverse change in compensation that does not affect other participants at the same level.* If the other Grunts cut the Grunt's GHRR by 50% but the others' GHRR stayed the same.

✓ *Relocation of the company more than 50 miles from its original location.* The Grunt may not be able to manage the commute. Extending the commute puts an unfair burden on the Grunt.

✓ *Death or disability.*

Sometimes the company chooses to change their strategy or they take on a new Grunt that has a particular set of skills that make another Grunt redundant. Or, perhaps they just don't like a Grunt even though the Grunt has worked hard and made a positive contribution. Companies, especially start-up companies, change fast and that means the herd must adapt and change as well. When this happens, however, you must still act fairly when dealing with the departing Grunt.

Whatever the reason, if the Grunt resigns with good cause, they should have an expectation of remuneration or pie that is more in line with their theoretical contribution.

In these cases the Grunt should be able to maintain their pie *minus* the amount of any severance payments made (if any). Subtract severance payments from their GHRR and recalculate the pie.

The company can choose to maintain a buyback option that would allow them to buyback the pie at the theoretical value (unadjusted) or fair value, whichever is higher. The buyback option should have a one-year protection clause that allows the departing Grunt to receive the full value of the shares if the company sells or goes public within 365 days after the buyback occurs. This will prevent the company from buying back the pie at the last minute before a liquidation event to turn a quick profit at the expense of the Grunt.

With regard to non-competition, the company is not entitled. The Grunt should be free to compete. If the company is concerned about this they should be more careful not to provide good cause for resignation. It's important to note, however, that *this does not mean the Grunt can steal ideas and intellectual property from the company,* even if the ideas were theirs. It does mean, however, that they can join a company in the same industry. For instance, if your company makes soda pop the departing Grunt can join a competitive soda pop company, but they can't take your secret formula, brands or other proprietary ideas.

This is fair treatment for a departing Grunt who left for circumstances outside his or her control. It is not fair to penalize a Grunt when he dedicated his time, energy and resources in good faith to the company. While it may not be ideal to have an absentee owner, it is much better than burning the Grunt and risking damage to your relationships with other members of the herd.

Death and Disability

If a Grunt becomes disabled she should be treated as Grunts who resigned for good cause. If the Grunt dies, his family should receive the full benefit of his contribution to the firm and they should be treated with as much respect as the Grunt himself.

Termination

When it's the company's decision to fire a Grunt it is called termination. Like resignation, termination can be with or without cause.

Termination Without Cause

These days business must change and adapt quickly. It is the job of the management team to make sure the right Grunts are in the right places. From time to time, however, the strategy changes and good, hardworking Grunts are no longer needed.

Several years ago I started a company and hired a staff of four to handle outbound telemarketing. I thought that telemarketing was the way to sell the product. It wasn't. The telemarketing Grunts worked hard and did their job, but I had to let them go. The company changed its strategy and no longer needed a herd of telemarketing Grunts. It wasn't their fault, it was mine.

When you terminate a Grunt without cause they should be treated the same way as if they left for good cause. This means they can retain their slice of the pie and even compete with you if they want (again, however, they can't take the company's intellectual property). While it might be more convenient for you if the Grunt didn't compete it wouldn't be fair. If you are concerned about competition then you should find a way to keep them in the herd.

Termination without cause must be handled extremely delicately. Nothing shows the true colors of a leader more than how they handle this situation.

I once knew a start-up where the CEO short-changed a Grunt who he terminated without cause. The Grunt had been faithful and had worked side-by-side with the CEO who had given him a lot of positive feedback for the Grunt's work.

However, the CEO was not a seasoned Grunt and he began to panic that the company wasn't an overnight success. He woke up one day and decided to let the hard-working Grunt go for no apparent reason.

The nasty CEO took back the equity the Grunt had vested by taking advantage of a loophole in the operating agreement even though it was clearly against the spirit of the contract.

Next, he withheld promised severance payments and slapped the Grunt with an oppressive non-compete agreement. The Grunt was mistreated and the other Grunts noticed. Morale sank, the company moved sideways for many months and they never got back on track.

The other Grunts saw the true colors of the leader and they began to question whether they would someday be treated unfairly themselves.

The CEO was unfair and selfish. He didn't understand that pies grew and he let greed steer his thoughts. By mistreating a Grunt in this manner he sent a clear message to the other Grunts that he didn't care about honoring the letter or the spirit of contracts and that he only cared about himself.

There is nothing more important than fair treatment. At the end of the day, all the money in the world won't make you a better person.

Termination With Cause

Sometimes the leader of the herd must fire a Grunt for cause. Generally speaking "cause" means one of the following:

✓ *Serious misconduct such as theft, dishonesty or assault.* Embezzlement, fighting, doing drugs or other illegal activity.

✓ *Habitual neglect of duty or incompetence.* For this to be cause, the participant has to clearly understand the requirements of the job, the requirements have to be reasonable given the resources of the company and a reasonable time period must be given for improvement.

✓ *Conduct incompatible with the employee's duties or prejudicial to the employer's business.* Engaging in activities during the workday that interfere with employment obligations or that compete with an employer's business is generally considered "cause". I once worked for an automotive company where one of the customer service people was ordering parts samples for his own use. Vendors would send them at no charge and the guy would take them home with him to put on his own car. This is unacceptable behavior. He was let go.

✓ *Willful disobedience* is another cause for termination. It means contempt or disrespect for individuals (especially superiors) or rules. It can also mean disobeying a reasonable and lawful request by the employer.

If the Grunt is terminated for cause, she should be treated the same as if she had resigned without cause. The company should recalculate her slice of the pie without the multipliers and the company should get a buyback right. Additionally, she should be required to sign a non-compete agreement in exchange for keeping their slice. Of course, if the Grunt embezzled money or otherwise sabotaged the business you may have a different set of legal problems. Even in these cases, fair treatment will keep you out of trouble.

How a manager handles termination for cause provides another peek into his or her true colors. Everyone in business should be treated with respect and dignity, no matter what.

I recently had coffee with a friend of mine who saw a mismanaged termination in his company and how it soured the attitudes of the whole heard. The manager was never really trusted again. To make matters worse, the manager became defensive whenever the terminated team member was mentioned in a positive way exacerbating the situation. The company never fully recovered.

Keep in mind that the company may have no legal obligation to anyone who leaves the company. But Slicing Pie isn't about what someone can legally get away with, it's about doing right by those who help you.

When we look at the world through only the legal lens we often overlook what is the right moral choice. Pie isn't equity, it's a promise. Promises should be kept.

For instance, the non-compete that you sign with a departing Grunt isn't a formal legal agreement, it's a reminder of the spirit of the Grunt Fund.

The right decision may not always be the most convenient, but in the long run I believe the company will be better off. Just because you can get away with something legally doesn't mean it's right.

Chapter Six:

The Magic Number

There are three situations in which you would want to stop using the Grunt Fund.

1. When you have built up so much theoretical value that you have reached a point of *diminishing returns*.
2. You have started to build an *actual business* model with predictable returns
3. The company receives a *cash investment* that is large enough to warrant legal and financial formalities.

The Point of Diminishing Returns

In the beginning a few hours of work might earn a significant slice of the pie. $100 in contributions against a $900 TBV would earn 10% of the pie. However, if your TBV is

$500,000 then your $100 incremental slice isn't much. This would be a good time to convert the pie to real equity.

Participants are no longer motivated by the incremental pie and new incentive program can be developed. Additionally, by the time this much work has gone into the pie you will know who the dedicated and valuable players are likely to be.

An Actual Business

Not all companies need to take on outside money. You may be smart or lucky enough to figure out how to grow your business based on revenues. In these cases the right time to stop using the Grunt Fund is when you have developed a predictable business model that looks like it's going to be a winner.

"Predictable" means that you have a revenue stream in the foreseeable future, you understand your basic cost structure and you have a plan for growth.

When you have this, you have a business that may have built actual value and you will need to hammer out the equity details more formally. This means calling your attorney, telling him or her how much pie everyone gets and asking them to put together an Operating Agreement or Shareholder's Agreement that will allow you to continue with your current team.

You may want to include some vesting or options program to help retain people, but make sure everyone who has earned pie is treated the same. It's not fair for you to change the rules on individual people. You can sometimes change the rules for the whole herd, but don't single anyone out. New employees can have a different deal. Keep in mind that if you later raise outside capital the new investors may put your equity in a vesting program even if it has already been issued.

Grunt Funds are best for early-stage companies that haven't built real value. By the time you actually do build value your team will be more or less solidified and new team members aren't really "founders" anymore so they can be offered an option program or a salary. You can then "freeze" the fund in preparation for the next phase of the business.

Your attorney will find it much easier to put together your agreements once the business is up and running with a bright future and a cohesive team. Equity splits won't be arbitrary, they will reflect real contributions.

Pie A La Mode

Grunt Fund-Friendly Lawyers
To find a Grunt Fund-friendly lawyer visit **SlicingPie.com** and click Pie à la Mode or scan the code.

Be sure to buy your lawyer a copy of Slicing Pie so they can create agreements that reflect the moral intent of the program. A good agreement will help guide good intentions. A bad agreement is a butt-covering tool that will allow mean people to take advantage of nice people.

Grunt Funds aren't for mean people.

Cash Investment

When you receive a significant investment all the Grunts will accept formal equity allocations based on the relative sizes of their slices of the pie. In some cases the investor will require the equity to be awarded in the form of options rather than straight equity. This is better for a number of reasons and worse for a number of reasons that I won't cover here. Just know that it is quite common for a formal investor to implement an option and/or vesting program.

Sometimes investors will impose some oppressive terms that seem unfair. The leader Grunt and other senior level Grunts will have to determine if it's worth it. Sometimes the company is desperate enough to have to take less-than-perfect investors. The important thing is that all Grunts get treated the same under the new investor terms.

You may be wondering how large the investment has to be to warrant legal and financial formalities.

The answer is *one million dollars.*

Rarely will you ever receive such a straight answer to a question like this in the start-up world. I, however, hate using the word "depends" so my answer is one million dollars. A million dollars isn't a huge amount of money, but it does set an actual value for the company and it does make incremental Grunt hours from employees a little less meaningful.

If your company receives a cash investment of at least one million dollars it is time to call in the lawyers and accountants and get everything documented and formalized. You will need to update your articles of incorporation, rewrite your operating agreement, prepare your investment documents and, in some cases, create employment agreements for Grunts who are about to become employees.

Don't be surprised if an investor who is bringing less than one million dollars to the table wants these things too. When this happens you will have to decide if it is worth it. The lawyers and accountants who do this kind of thing will charge you somewhere in the neighborhood of $15,000 - $50,000 for a very bare bones package. I would rather use that kind of money to get customers, but I completely understand if an investor wants to have the right agreements in place. Investors want to protect their money because it's hard to get and everybody wants some.

If the money is coming in at less than one million dollars it might be easier to call it a convertible loan and be done with it. That way the cash can turn into equity when you do get someone willing to pony up a cool million or more. To provide security to the investor the key Grunts can personally guarantee the loan.

The amount of equity that the one million dollars buys will be based on the negotiated pre-money value, or what I call the "Magic Number". It is the value that is high enough to motivate the Grunts to keep working and low enough to motivate the investor to invest. If the Magic Number is higher than the theoretical value of the contribution by the various Grunts everyone should be happy!

If your Magic Number is too low you and the other Grunts won't walk away from the transaction with very much equity and your motivation will dip. If your Magic Number is too high the investors will look elsewhere for a better deal. Unfortunately for you, there is no shortage of potential deals for investors.

You don't have to bring up the Grunt Fund and the TBV with potential investors. It has no bearing on actual value, so discussing it will only complicate things. At this point in the game you want to get the best deal for you and your fellow Grunts. When the investor comes on board they will be your team member so be sure to be fair in your dealings with them as well.

In the scheme of things one million dollars isn't really that much money. How much of the pie the Grunts are able to share depends on how good they are a demonstrating value.

When you are starting to talk about real money your lawyer-dollars will be well spent.

Lawyers and accountants will save you from a lot of headaches down the road now that you have actually baked a tasty pie!

Chapter Seven:

Grunt Fund Recap

The most common mistakes entrepreneurs make when allocating equity is slicing the pie *before* it is baked or slicing the pie *after* is it baked. Neither way takes into account the ever-changing needs of a fledgling business.

To make matters worse, most people use a fixed-split method for equity which inevitably leads to uncomfortable renegotiations when the company changes.

A Grunt Fund is a fair and equitable way to allocate equity in an early-stage start-up company. It is a method for implementing a dynamic equity split for you and your fellow Grunts.

To employ the method simply track the theoretical value of the various ingredients that Grunts contribute in order to bake the pie.

Ingredients include:

✓ Time
✓ Money, in the form of cash or cash equivalents
✓ Supplies and equipment that enable the business
✓ Relationships
✓ Intellectual property

In a Grunt Fund, Grunts are given pie in proportion to their contribution to the overall theoretical value.

Occasionally early Grunts can "harvest" some of the value they have created by calibrating the theoretical value to a higher number. The new value becomes the base against which they (and new Grunts entering the herd) will earn additional pie.

Care must be taken to ensure that the new, calibrated amount does not over estimate what the actual value of the company will eventually be. If it does, the Grunts will be unhappy.

As an alternative to calibration, the Grunts can "partition" off part of the pie and split up the rest. Their partitioned percentage remains fixed while the rest changes based on inputs from the herd.

When a Grunt resigns *without cause* or is terminated *with cause* they should not expect to get any pie at the theoretical value of their contributions. At best, they should be entitled to a slice based on an adjusted value that is set equal to the actual value of cash or cash equivalents. The company should be able to maintain a buyback option for the pie.

When a Grunt resigns *with good cause*, is terminated *without cause*, becomes disabled, or dies, the Grunt should expect to keep their slice of the pie at the theoretical value less any severance payments.

The company can choose to maintain a buyback provision at an amount equal to the theoretical value or the fair value, whichever is higher. The buyback should provide full value of the shares if there is a significant liquidation event within one year of the buyback.

A Grunt Fund, at its core, is about treating people fairly. While most entrepreneurs are motivated by money at some level, they are also motivated by being part of the game, working as a team and building something from scratch. Being a Grunt takes dedication and commitment. It's a hard life but the rewards are great—even if the company isn't successful. The evidence is that many Grunts jump right back in to start-ups after leaving failed start-ups. They can't get enough.

It is possible, and indeed common, for entrepreneurs to bite the hand that feeds them by burning hardworking Grunts. Sometimes this is intentional and sometimes it's because they lack the tools and the understanding to execute a fair model—now they have one.

If you bake it, they will come…

Chapter Eight:

Retrofitting a Grunt Fund

If you have already launched your business chances are good that you have already implemented a fixed split that is causing some angst among the founders. You now need to unwind your fixed split so you can get on the right track with your equity. This will require you to retrofit the Grunt Fund. Retrofitting a Grunt Fund is fairly easy as long as everyone is willing to cooperate.

Getting Buy-In from the Herd

The first thing you will need to do is get everyone on board with the program by helping them see the benefit of a dynamic equity split program. To do this, just give them a copy of this book.

The people on your team will fall into two

categories:

1. "Skinny Grunts" are those who have *less* than they deserve
2. "Fat Grunts" are those who have *more* than they deserve

(It is unlikely that anyone will have *exactly* what they deserve.)

The Skinny Grunts will be easy to convince. They already feel cheated by the Fat Grunts and, as much as they might like the business and believe in the vision, their motivation is probably waning because they feel like they are working for someone else's benefit.

The Fat Grunts may be harder to convince because after the retrofit they will probably have a smaller portion of equity and they will have to start working to maintain or grow their position in the company. This, of course, is completely fair.

In most cases, if they have this book, they should be on board by the time they read this section. If not, I have a message for them:

Dear Fat Grunt,

Your current share of the equity that you hold in this business is disproportionate to what you actually deserve and it is now threatening your relationships with other team members and probably destroying the company. The company will be more valuable if you realign your interests with the rest of the team. Unless you are willing to be fair about what you and everyone deserves you will limit the chances that your company will be successful and that shares will ever be worth anything. Please cooperate with the rest of your team to ensure that you and your fellow Grunts get the right amount of equity.

Most sincerely,

Mlih M.

Mike Moyer, Grunt

If that doesn't work, you are probably dealing with someone who has trust or greed issues. Either way they are not properly aligned with the team. This is a good time to fire them.

You need to work with people that you can trust. You can't trust people who aren't willing to treat you and the other members of the team fairly. A greedy Fat Grunt is someone who is comfortable benefiting at the expense of others. There is a word for people like this; the word is "asshole." It's is best not to do business with assholes. You can probably find someone else to do that Grunt's job

Some Grunts, like those who have controlling interest in the company, own the core intellectual property or have large amounts of cash invested, are difficult to replace.

If you are dealing with an irreplaceable Grunt you may have to cut your losses and leave the company yourself. There are greener pastures for a good Grunt.

Such are the problems with fixed-split

equity program. Next time you will be older and wiser and can start a Grunt Fund from the beginning. I hope you will not have this problem.

The Retrofit

Once you get everyone on board with the program you will have to calculate what the pie *would* have looked like *if* you had been using a Grunt Fund from day one. This will require you to do an inventory of the various contributions that people have made and add it all up to determine your TBV. Time will be the most difficult because in most cases people will not have been tracking their time very accurately.

Time Tracking

At this point it will be impractical for everyone to remember how many hours they contributed. It will be easier to divide people into full-time, half-time and part-time.

Count the number of weeks people have been involved and use 40-50 hours per week for full time employees, 20 hours per week for half time employees and 10 hours per week for part time employees. Do your best, but don't split hairs—it's not worth it.

The Pie

Once you figure out what the pie should look like all of the participants in the Grunt Fund will simply continue earning pie according to the regular rules. Things will proceed as described in this book. At some point you will outgrow the Grunt Fund and you will want to issue actual stock and work with your lawyer to put the right agreements in place.

When you issue stock (in an LLC they may be called "participation shares" or "units" or something like that) you simply issue enough shares to bring everyone to the right percentages.

Example:

Grunt 1 and Grunt 2 start a company together and split the equity "50/50" they authorize 100 shares in the company and each take 50 shares.

A few months go by and it becomes obvious that Grunt 1 isn't very interested in the business. They agree to retrofit a Grunt Fund to solve the problem.

They go back and tally up each of their contributions since the beginning and determine that if they had been using a Grunt Fund from day one Grunt 1 would have about 25% of the pie and Grunt 2 would have 75% of the pie. (At this point it doesn't really matter what stock has been issued because the stock is worthless anyway.) From that point on they earn pie under the terms of the Grunt Fund.

When Grunt 3 joins the herd she starts earning pie under the terms of the Grunt Fund.

Simple as pie.

Six months go by and the team is getting some traction in the market. They are generating some nice revenue and they have outgrown the Grunt Fund. Grunt 1 has about 30% of the pie, Grunt 2 has 60% of the pie and Grunt 3 has 10% of the pie. They decide to issue 69 shares of stock to allocate the proper percentages.

Remember, Grunts 1 and 2 already each have 50 shares. So, Grunt 1 gets zero new shares, Grunt 2 gets 52 shares and Grunt 3 (who had zero) gets 17 shares. When the new stock is granted the ownership looks like this:

	Had	Gets	Has	
Grunt 1	50	0	50	30%
Grunt 2	50	52	102	60%
Grunt 3	0	17	17	10%
	100	69	169	

The Grunt Fund has properly allocated shares to the right people. Each Grunt has a share that is fair relative to the other Grunts. The original allocations had no impact on the outcome because the additional stock grants balanced things out appropriately.

Grunt 2, who originally owned 50% of the company now owns 30%. He has nothing to be sad about; the company is now worth much more than before. If he had decided to be an Asshole the company probably would have fallen apart.

A Note about Fat Grunts

Not all Fat Grunts are assholes. In some cases a Grunt is *intentionally* fat because they used the partitioning or calibration technique I mentioned before. This is fine as long as all the other Grunts are aware of the situation.

These techniques allow very early founders to benefit from their early work in the company. As long as they are playing by the rules, all is fair and square.

Chapter Nine:

Going Out of Business

There are two main reasons why an early stage start-up fails. The first is that the company goes bankrupt because it can't meet its financial obligations. The second is that the founders learn enough about the market to decide that it's not really as cool as they initially thought.

Bankruptcy

Sometimes your fledgling company will rack up some serious debt and, before you know it, you are all underwater. Unless your company is generating enough cash to service the debt you will need a way to come up with payments.

As I mentioned before, when a Grunt personally secures debt on behalf of the company it will not translate into pie so long as the debt is being serviced by the company. However, if the company cannot cover payments, the individual who guaranteed the credit is now responsible for covering the payment him or herself. In these cases the payments are treated as cash contributions for which the theoretical value is four times the amount of the payment (which doesn't matter much if the company is going under but oh well…)

Usually the debt is taken on by a senior participant. Rarely, if ever, should the company use credit supplied by a junior member of the team.

If the company has secured the credit on its own and cannot cover the payments, it must look for cash contributions. In some cases, members of the herd can come to the rescue. In other cases you can invite an outside investor. Unfortunately, outside investors rarely want to bail a start-up company out of debt. This is a pretty bad use of funds.

It would be tempting to "pass the hat" or allocate the debt across participants according to their share of equity. This is a bad idea. Grunts don't want to be put in a position where they have to cough up their own money. They work for pie. Pie will become equity. Equity is an asset. Grunts do not work for liabilities. If they think their job is turning into a liability they will resign.

Sometimes you'll see the pass-the-hat scene in movies where the employees and friends come to the aid of their fearless leader who has fallen on hard times. But this isn't really how it happens outside of Bedford Falls. Sometimes it just ain't a wonderful life.

This is one of those cases where the leadership of the organization will have to take the hit. They will have to cover the company's debt and their payments will be treated as cash.

If leadership is not willing or able to cover the debt they may have to close the business. When you close the business you would sell whatever assets you have, pay off the debt and distribute what is left to Grunts based on their slice of the pie (more on this in a minizzle.)

Less Cool

After giving it the old college try, the founders may decide that they were wrong about the market and it's not going to be the cakewalk they envisioned to change the world in the manner they had originally planned.

Maybe they couldn't get the product to work. Maybe they underestimated the competition. Maybe their spouses wanted them to find a real job. Maybe they just decided the idea wasn't that great after all.

Maybe it was just too hard…

The world seems to be designed in a way that success is never as easy as we hope. Getting there takes not only the right vision, but also the right level of perseverance that some people just don't have.

Passing the Pie to Other Grunts

When it's time to depart, the founders of the company could decide to pass the pie off to fellow Grunts. In this the case they can resign, just like any other Grunt. They will be treated like any other resignation without cause and leadership will pass to the next largest shareholder (or whatever the herd decides).

If none of the other Grunts wants to carry on you may have to sell what you can and shut down the company.

Shutting Down

If the company's debt exceeds any cash they were able to generate through the sale of assets the company will still owe the creditors. If you anticipated taking on the debt you should have set up a legal structure, such as an LLC, to protect the herd's personal possessions. It is likely that the creditors will come after you directly, but you might be okay if you structured the company legally. If you did not set up a corporate structure the creditors will come after whoever they can. *I'm not recommending that you try to avoid your debts.* Usually debt is owed by individuals within the herd. They are ultimately responsible for paying it off.

When it is time to close the doors the assets in the business should be sold and debts repaid. If there is any cash leftover it should be distributed in the following order:

1. Grunts that put in cash or cash equivalents should be paid back in an amount equal to their contribution. This payback will not diminish their equity holding, however (if it matters).

2. If there is not enough cash to cover the cash contributions then payments in proportion to the cash contributions should be made. So, divide an individual Grunt's cash contributions and divide by the total cash contributions and give them that percent of the leftover cash.

3. If there is any cash left over it should be distributed to all the Grunts according to their percent of equity.

The goal is to make everyone as whole again as possible. Legal creditors (including personal credit cards) always get first rights to the cash. Anyone who put in cash took larger risks and care should be taken to preserve their cash. Grunts, as Grunts, knew getting into this thing that they might not get paid so anything is better than nothing in a going-out-of-business situation.

Chapter Ten:

Legalize It!

The first rule of business, especially entrepreneurship, is to work with people you can trust. A Grunt Fund is the foundation of a trusting relationship. If your first instinct is to protect yourself against your fellow Grunts, you have probably chosen the wrong herd.

A Grunt Fund documents fair treatment and provides a starting point for a group of like-minded people with a common vision to start a company without a lot of hassle. However, even if you engage a Grunt Fund-friendly attorney to help you set up some basic contracts, it is quite possible that you can join a Grunt Fund and still get burned.

If you want to avoid getting burned, you will probably be disappointed as an entrepreneur. You can't cover your butt from all possible risk.

Without a Net

Hiring lawyers and accountants to set up your company agreements and legal structures isn't free. Most of the good lawyers I know provide deep discounts for start-ups as long as they are doing basic things. Still, I'd rather see entrepreneurs spend their money on marketing and sales. Aside from setting up some basic liability protection (more below), try to avoid spending money on too much legal stuff until you are confident that your company has legs.

In the very early days of a new company your focus should be on proof of concept and nothing else. Spend your time and money finding out if there are people in the world that are interested in buying your product or service.

In some cases, moving forward without legal protection is your only option. Going without a net is riskier, but then again, you may not fall and everything will turn out okay.

With a Net

If you discover there are people out there who want to spend money on your product you may be on to something. It's now time to mitigate the possibility of getting burned by setting up some basic legal structures to help organize and protect your company. Keep in mind, however, that to most lawyers and accountants a Grunt Fund will be a fairly novel concept. Most are used to doing it the traditional way so it's probably a good idea to either hire a Grunt Fund-friendly lawyer or make sure the lawyer you hire is up to speed with the concepts in this book.

What to Talk to Your Lawyer About

To help you get the most out of your Grunt-Funded company you will want to discuss liability, ownership rights and taxation with your lawyer.

One of the first things you will want to do with your new company is to set up a formal corporate structure. In most cases, you can set up the company yourself using online tools or going directly to the Secretary of State. I like this method because it requires more research which helps you better understand how it all works. However, most start-up friendly lawyers will help you set up your company at a very reasonable rate. Grunt Fund-friendly lawyers may even take pie instead of cash.

Limiting Liability

A key feature of any formal business structure is its ability to protect the owner's personal assets from liabilities incurred by the company. This includes everything from corporate debt to lawsuits. The protection they offer isn't always bulletproof, but it's better than nothing. The better you manage and organize the business the more protection it will provide. For the most part this means a clear separation between personal activities and the activities of the company. Avoid turning business trips into vacations and avoid dipping into corporate bank accounts for personal reasons.

When you meet with your lawyer be sure to discuss ways to get the most protection from your legal entity.

Ownership Rights

Setting up a formal corporate structure will also help you manage intellectual property rights and asset ownership. When a Grunt makes a contribution to the company the Grunt relinquishes ownership of that contribution to the company. This is important because you don't want people taking things out of the company when and if they leave. If you start a pizza shop and your partner contributes a pizza oven in exchange for pie, the company should own the oven. If you don't have a formal entity set up the guy can bail and take his oven with him. That wouldn't be very good, raw pizzas aren't very delicious.

Likewise, if the team writes some great software the company should own the code. You don't want individuals to take copies with them and build competing firms.

It's better that the company owns all the stuff and all the intellectual property by default. This is a general rule for all companies, not just those with Grunt Funds.

Taxation

This is where things get interesting. How you and your company get taxed has everything to do with the type of formal entity you set you. Most people reading this book will be deciding between and Limited Liability Company (LLC) or a Corporation (Inc).

LLCs are Better

LLCs are a good choice for Grunt-Funded companies because they offer more overall flexibility than corporations.

One of the best features of the LLC is that partners in an LLC can divide up the profits anyway they want. Using a Grunt Fund you could simply distribute profits according to each person's share of the pie (this assumes that each person receiving profits has at least nominal ownership in the company). This can change whenever you want so as the pie changes so does the payout.

Things get a little more complicated if you decide to liquidate the company or transfer ownership to a buyer or investor. While the founders were sharing profits, each was earning "credit" in his or her capital account which will ultimately determine how the proceeds are distributed. You should be okay as long as you were following the rules. Each person's capital account should reflect their share of the pie. Talk

to your lawyer about what all these things mean –
I'm not entirely sure myself.

Corporations are Trickier, But Not Impossible

A corporation is a good choice if you expect that
your start-up will require significant investment in
the short term. Stock in a corporation is more
structured and VCs and sophisticated Angel
investors often prefer this structure.

Keep in mind that it is fairly easy to
convert an LLC to a corporation, but it's hard to
convert a corporation to an LLC. So, starting
with an LLC is a good idea.

The problem with corporations (S-corps
or C-corps) is that the IRS assumes the "normal"
method of dividing up the pie before it's baked
because that's how it usually happens. If Grunts
receive equity after it's baked (based on their
percentage of the pie) the IRS might argue that
the stock was essentially compensation that can
be taxed as regular income.

To avoid this problem the equity needs to
be granted early in the process when the value is
clearly zero. This, unfortunately, creates a fixed
split.

To solve the problem you will want to
issue restricted stock to Grunts that is subject to
vesting and buyback provisions that mirror the
concepts in this book. Each Grunt will need to
file an 83(b) election with the IRS which helps
ensure there will be no tax when the stock
eventually vests (ask your lawyer about this).

Example:

Clint and Chuck go into business together selling Abraham Lincoln action figures. They form a C-corporation and each take 1,000 shares of restricted stock subject to Grunt Fund-style vesting and buyback provisions. Both of them file 83(b) elections with the IRS.

   After the first month, Clint has earned 80% of the pie and Chuck has 20%. Eight of Clint's shares vest and two of Chuck's vest, so they now own 80% and 20% respectively.

	Restricted Shares	Previously Vested	Current Vest	Total Vested	
Clint	1,000	0	8	8	80%
Chuck	1,000	0	2	2	20%
	2,000	0	10	10	

   The following month they hire Parker. They issue 1,000 shares of restricted stock to him subject to the same terms. Parker files an 83(b) election as well.

   At the end of the next month, Clint has 70% of the pie, Chuck has 20% and Parker has 10%. The shares vest to bring their vested shares in alignment with the pie: 12 more of Clint's shares vest, four more of Chuck's shares vest and three of Parker's vest. So, at the end of the second month Clint has 20 vested shares, Chuck has six vested shares and Parker has three. Their vested shares equals the pie.

	Restricted Shares	Previously Vested	Current Vest	Total Vested	
Clint	1,000	8	12	20	70%
Chuck	1,000	2	4	6	20%
Parker	1,000	0	3	3	10%
	3,000	10	19	29	

It doesn't matter how many shares each person has, it only matters what percent they have vested. Each period you simply vest whatever is necessary to bring everyone in line.

The next month Chuck decides that he no longer wants to be involved. He is leaving without good reason. His shares are subject to a buyback provision that reflects the spirit of the Grunt Fund. His shares are taken back by the company and the remaining founders (Clint and Parker) are the only outstanding shareholders.

	Restricted Shares	Previously Vested	Current Vest	Total Vested	
Clint	1,000	20	0	20	87%
Parker	1,000	3	0	3	13%
	2,000	23	0	23	

The remaining shares reflect the percent ownership for each participant. Both Grunts have a larger share, but they have been left in the lurch by the departing Grunt so they will have to scramble to rebuild their company.

A Grunt Fund-style vesting schedule is considerably more complicated than a traditional vesting schedule. In a traditional program a certain number of shares vests after certain periods of time or certain events. In the Grunt-Fund-style program the contract will have to reflect the terms of the Grunt Fund. It is not an insurmountable legal problem. If your lawyer tries to talk you out of using a Grunt Fund you are dealing with someone who does not fully appreciate the concept. Find someone who does.

I can help connect you with a Grunt Fund-friendly lawyer. I keep tabs on lawyers who have embraced the Grunt Fund concept. Some of them have even started developing some boiler-plate Grunt Fund contracts that I'll post to my site.

A special thanks to Clint Costa, Esq. who provided the inspiration for this chapter.

Pie A La Mode

Grunt Fund-Friendly Lawyers
To find a Grunt Fund-friendly lawyer visit **SlicingPie.com** and click Pie à la Mode or scan the code.

Chapter Eleven:

Making Grunt Funds Work

The essential ingredient in a good pie is *fairness*. People deserve to be treated fairly no matter what. Greed, which is the desire to have more than you deserve, is the enemy of fairness. Gordon Gekko's famous line "greed is good," does not work well in a start-up environment.

My parents taught me that life isn't fair, and that's true. This book isn't going to change that. Notice, however, that when you get the short end of the stick you often feel resentment toward those who put you in that situation.

You don't want those people to be your teammates in your start-up company. Those kinds of relationships are difficult to repair.

In order for a start-up to succeed you need to create a high level of trust. Leaders need to earn trust and maintain it. Otherwise the company will decay and any success will be dumb luck.

To make the Grunt Fund work you will first need to share the rules with everyone and agree to follow them. That's where this book can come in handy.

If you disagree with my rules as outlined here that's fine. Make up your own rules. As long as they are fair and everyone agrees to them in advance you have the foundation of a Grunt Fund.

Perhaps you think that cash shouldn't get four times its value in pie. No problem. Change it. Just make sure you don't change the rules in the middle of the game. The rules in this book are based on my own experience. Yours may be different.

Ultimately a Grunt Fund is about you and your fellow Grunts. Create rules that you are comfortable with that will allow you to move forward with a common understanding. A Grunt Fund is kind of its own philosophy. Sometimes you have to think issues through and have discussions about what you feel is right and wrong. Have the discussions and do your thinking before problems arise.

The real danger is not having rules at all or not settling on them in advance. Start-ups are fast-changing environments, but not everything should change on the fly. If you must change a rule, be sure to get every Grunts input. Do not take changes lightly; bad changes can poison a good herd of Grunts.

How I Can Help

I'm on a mission to make sure that all entrepreneurs get what they deserve from their hard work. My job won't be done until every start-up uses a dynamic equity split program like a Grunt Fund.

When you have questions or concerns about your own Grunt Fund I would be happy to help you figure out what the right "Slicing Pie" decision should be. Just let me know when you run into snags.

If you are part of an incubator, accelerator or other entrepreneurial organization I would be happy to do seminars or webinars for your members. I'm happy to do anything I can do to help start-ups and spread the word.

How You Can Help

There are lots of entrepreneurs, just like you, who are struggling with how to properly reward their team. If you like this book please review it on Amazon, email it, tweet it, blog it, or otherwise share it with people in your network. They, and I, will appreciate it!

Also, I occasionally update this book based on feedback from readers. If you have ideas for improving the content in this book please let me know. The legal and retrofit chapters, for example, were written as a direct response to reader comments. I've also created

"A La Mode" content to help readers with specific problems.

When you use a Grunt Fund you are being fair to your team and to yourself. Remember, fairness is fun! So have fun, I wish you nothing but success beyond your wildest dreams.

Most sincerely,

Mike Moyer
mike@SlicingPie.com
July, 2013

Version 2.3

Leave a Review

Slicing Pie on Amazon.com
If you liked Slicing Pie, please leave a review on Amazon.com, I would really appreciate it! Scan the code to link to the review page.

Part II:

Grunt Funds in Action

The following case studies are designed to help enlighten you with regard to the practical application of a Grunt Fund.

All the examples and case studies are fictional (just like most financial projections). I'll create more fictional case studies and post them on SlicingPie.com, please feel free to bring me your own problems and stories.

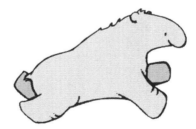

Grunt Funds are all about action.

The Case of:

John's Bicycle Attic, LLC

John loves bikes and wants to start a bike repair service. He tells his friend Mike and they decide to start a bike repair shop in their basement and call it John's Bicycle Attic and use a Grunt Fund to slice the pie.

The only other job that either of them had was when they were dish dogs at the local country club. John, who was a dish dog longer than Mike, earned $10.00 per hour and Mike only earned $9.00 per hour.

They appoint John as the president of the company because it was his idea and he has the most bike-repair experience.

John provides a repair stand and a killer set of tools that enable the business.

Over the next month John works 100 hours in the shop and Mike works 100 hours talking to bike owners and generating business.

Mike spends $1,000 on flyers and ads for the company and he brings $100 in snacks for the shop from his home. He does not expect to be reimbursed.

When using a Grunt Fund the first step is to figure out John and Mike's Grunt Hourly Resource Rate (GHRR). Because they were hourly workers before, it's okay to double their previous rate for their GHRR. This would give John a GHRR of $20.00 and Mike a GHRR of $18.00. Mike and John, however, are smart guys. They realize that fixing bikes isn't the same as washing dishes and they agree they have complementary skills. So, they agree to take an equal GHRR of $20/hour. You don't have to split hairs with a Grunt Fund. They keep it real.

Next, they have to take John's equipment into account. Because the equipment enables the business it should be assigned a theoretical value. John didn't buy the tools specifically for the business so they looked up a comparable set of tools on Ebay.com and found some for around $1,000. So, the theoretical value of the business enabling equipment is $1,000.

Mike also contributed to the business with supplies consisting of flyers, for which he paid $1,000, and snacks, for which he paid $100.

The snacks, which he brought from home, are business facilitating supplies and should not be assigned a value. They are nice to have, but not critical. The flyers, on the other hand, were a business expense for which Mike does not expect to be reimbursed. The theoretical value of that contribution is the amount of cash times four.

So, at the end of the first month John would own 33% of the pie and Mike would own 67%

	John	Mike	
Time	2,000	2,000	
Equipment	1,000	-	
Cash (x4)	-	4,000	Total
	$3,000	$6,000	$9,000
	33%	67%	

In the above example, the Grunt Model has properly divided the pie of the business among the two partners. Over the next month the partner's commitments change.

Mike gets a new girlfriend, Anne, and starts spending a lot of time over at her apartment. Over the next month he only spends 50 hours promoting the business and spends no money on advertising. John spends 75 hours in the shop and 75 hours generating business. He also spends $500 on advertising.

At the end of the second month, John has committed 175 hours, $1,000 in enabling equipment and $500 on advertising. His total theoretical value has grown to $8,000. Mike has committed 150 hours and $1,000 on advertising. Hit total theoretical value has grown to $7,000. At the end of the second month John's slice of the pie is 53% and Mike's is 47%.

	John	Mike	
Time	5,000	3,000	
Equipment	1,000	-	
Cash (x4)	2,000	4,000	Total
	$8,000	$7,000	$15,000
	53%	47%	

As you can see, John's pie slice grows to reflect his dedication to the business. If John and Mike had simply split the business 50/50 in the beginning there would no doubt be hard feelings among the partners. In this model the allocation is fair based on the personal choices of the two participants.

Mike continues to spend time with his smokin'-hot girlfriend instead of building the business so they decide to add a third partner, Sam. Sam ran a bike shop for many years before selling it. His experience will add a lot to the business.

Sam's last salary at a bike shop was $50,000 per year. Sam agrees to the Grunt Model and starts work. Over the next month Mike spends 20 hours promoting the business, John spends 150 hours in the shop and Sam spends 50 hours in the shop and 50 hours calling his old customers and generating a lot of business

Under the Grunt Model, Sam can slip right in and start earning pie. At $50,000 per year his GHRR is $50.00. John and Mike think this is fair given the fact that he has far more experience than either of them. At the end of the third month the pie split is as follows:

	John	Mike	Sam	
Time	8,000	3,400	2,500	
Equipment	1,000			
Cash (x4)	2,000	4,000		Total
	$11,000	$7,400	$2,500	$20,900
	53%	35%	12%	100%

The Grunt Fund has provided a method for adding another partner in a fair and consistent manner. The theoretical base value has grown and all parties have a fair share.

Removing a Partner

In the above example, it seems that Mike's commitment is waning and he may be on his way out. At such an early stage, it would be impractical for Mike to keep his pie in spite of his contribution. Investors don't look favorably on absentee-owners.

While Mike has added value to the business and it should not be overlooked, it is clear that the young company has a long way to go and unless Mike sticks with it, he may not be entitled to the gains. There are three scenarios in which Mike can depart the business. Each one creates special circumstances that need to be considered if he is to be treated fairly. The three scenarios are:

1. Mike can quit, also called resignation without cause

2. Mike can be "pushed out", also called resignation with good cause or termination without cause

3. Mike can be fired, also called termination with cause

Starting a new business is precarious and commitment of the partners is important. Half-hearted commitment can damage a business beyond repair. An understanding, in advance, of expectations can help pave the way to a successful transition without hard feelings.

Resignation without Cause

If Mike quits for personal reasons—resignation without cause—then he will have to accept a reduced slice of the pie and give the company the opportunity to buy it back. If the company cannot buy back the equity, the Grunt Fund after Mike's departure looks like this:

	John	Mike	Sam	
Time	8,000		2,500	
Equipment	1,000			
Cash (x4)	2,000	1,000		Total
	$ 11,000	$ 1,000	$ 2,500	$ 14,500
	76%	7%	17%	100%

The Grunt Model has fairly resized the slices. Mike now receives $0 per hour worked instead of $20 and his cash contribution does not get the 4x multiplier.

Notice that the total theoretical value of the pie has gone from $20,900 down to $14,500. This is not a problem. Remember, the company still has no actual value so this number is simply used to help define the relative size of the Grunts' slices. It really doesn't matter what the number is as long as it helps us keep track of the inputs.

Both John and Sam now have a larger share of the pie. That doesn't necessarily mean they are better off. They no longer have Mike and they may have to find someone new.

Mike shouldn't feel too bad. The company just wasn't for him. He still has some pie, but the company can buy it back. It is important to remember that we are not dealing with actual stock with actual value. When I say "buyback" I'm really talking about the company paying back Mike's cash. Remember, slices in the pie are nothing except a personal promise from the founder to provide an equity cut at some point in the future.

If John, as the founder, does not want to give any pie to Mike he has several choices. The first is to blow off Mike and not keep his promise. This happens all the time, but it's not fair.

The other thing John could do is give $1,000 of his own money to pay back Mike for the expenses he incurred and the time he spent. John would then own Mike's pie at the 4x rate.

Or, if the company had $1,000 they could cut a check from the company account to cover the expenses.

Mike should be happy with any of these deals. They are all fair.

Termination without Cause or Resignation with Good Cause

Let's pretend that Mike liked working for the business, but couldn't dedicate much time to the effort and his lack of dedication bothers John and Sam.

John and Sam could simply ask him to leave. He did his job, he helped build the business, but they need someone more reliable. No hard feelings.

In this case, it would be fair for the company to either do a buyout or allow Mike to keep his pie with a buyback option.

If the company chooses to do a buyout, the Mike would be entitled to the theoretical value of his pie.

Notice that this option is expensive. They will have to come up with $4,000 to pay back the $1,000 that Mike invested. This is perfectly fair. Mike didn't actually do anything wrong, the other Grunts just wanted to replace him. It's okay for them to want someone else, but they can't penalize Mike for no reason.

This kind of agreement creates a little job security for Grunts because herd members will need to think twice before they act on a whim and let someone go without cause.

Likewise, if John and Sam told Mike that

he wasn't going to get paid as much (but they were keeping their rates), or if they told him that he was no longer in charge of marketing, Mike could resign for good reason with the same benefits as if he had been terminated without cause.

Termination with Cause

If Mike had been repeatedly asked to perform certain duties and he did not, John may have a cause to fire him. In this case it would count as a termination with cause and Mike would not be entitled to some of the pie.

Mike would forfeit the pie earned through his hours worked as well as any unpaid commissions he would have received in pie.

The cash Mike put in would be recalculated to match the actual value of the cash without the multiplier. The company does not have to pay this back, but will have to issue equity when the time comes. If the equity is issued then there should be a one-year protection as discussed before.

John's Bicycle Attic Survives

As you can see, because John's Bicycle Attic is using a Grunt Fund, the pie adjusts as the business changes and it is clear what happens under different scenarios.

In all of the above scenarios, Mike is

treated fairly. He gets what he deserves. Because he is a friend and fellow Grunt, he should be treated fairly no matter what.

The Case of:

PhoneMatcherator.com, LLC

Sally was a successful businesswoman who made her fortune selling helicopters to other successful businesswomen and men. She also had a short stint as the CEO of an online company that sold cell phones during the dot-com bubble and did quite well. She had gone back into the helicopter business when she had an idea. The idea was to match people with the right cell phone after they answered a few questions. The idea wasn't terribly original, but Sally thought it was and wanted to give it a shot.

Sally put together a little PowerPoint outline of her idea and shared it with Frank, a career entrepreneur who had a lot of experience with online companies and, although he had started several tech companies, he hadn't been as fortunate as Sally, who could retire if she wanted to.

Frank, who didn't have a big nest egg, told Sally he was interested in helping her start the company but he would need to earn a salary in addition to equity. Sally agreed and offered him $100,000 (which was half what he was paid in his previous position) plus 10% of the equity vesting over five years.

She asked Frank to sign a complicated non-compete and non-disclosure agreement along with an employment agreement that provided severance payments and accelerated vesting of shares in the event that Frank was forced out of the company.

Sally also took $100,000 in salary but agreed to let the money accrue instead of being paid. She often reminded the other staff members that she was not being paid current compensation- she mentioned this often in hopes of motivating them (it didn't).

Over the next few months Frank worked 60-70 hours per week and relocated his family so he could be closer to the office. Sally worked part-time on the business and invested about $250,000 of her own money. Frank brainstormed with Sally, wrote the business plan and the software specification, hired the staff, and began to execute.

Sally spent thousands of dollars on lawyers and accountants who made sure all the contracts were neat and covered the appropriate asses, which, for the most part meant Sally's ass. Rather than building a culture of trust, Sally built contracts.

With Frank at the helm, the company successfully launched the site on time and within budget. Sally was very happy with Frank and gave him plenty of positive feedback and relied on him for most of the execution while she played more of a strategic role. They were a good team and built a good company.

PhoneMatcherator.com grew steadily over the next two years and was meeting its projections; however, Sally grew frustrated that the company didn't perform as well as the company she ran during the dot-com bubble. She didn't realize that it was a different time and her company wasn't the only company that sold phones online. Today there are hundreds of resellers.

To make matters worse, a competitor had launched shortly after them and was growing neck-and-neck with PhoneMatcherator.com

Sally was still selling helicopters on the side. She began to worry that the company wouldn't be the overnight sensation that she had dreamed about and, on a whim, she terminated Frank without cause. Frank was shocked. He had received excellent feedback and had trusted her completely. She offered little explanation to her action other than she had "lost confidence" in his abilities.

Under the terms of his employment agreement, Frank was entitled to severance payments and accelerated vesting of part of his equity. Sally held out on the severance payments and, taking advantage of a small loophole in the company's operating agreement, she took back all the equity that Frank had earned over the past two years including the shares that vested under the employment agreement leaving Frank with nothing. After making Frank sign a broad and oppressive separation agreement, Sally paid him the severance payment that she owed.

Over the next few months the company's growth plateaued. They continued to burn through their start-up fund and the other employees, who missed Frank, began to lose their passion for the business. After seeing how Sally treated Frank, a loyal employee, they began to look for other jobs fearing that they would meet the same fate.

When Sally hired a new person, Sue, to replace Frank she made her sign a bunch of contracts. Sue found out that Sally hadn't honored the contracts with Frank so she didn't trust what she was signing. She and Sally had to create tighter contracts to eliminate loopholes. It was expensive and time consuming.

By the time Sue got started the team had been hearing about all the legal work it took to get her on board and they resented her for spending so much time and money. They were fragile anyway. They also missed Frank which made Sue's job even harder.

The above example shows what can happen when entrepreneurs don't use a Grunt Fund. Sally makes a number of important mistakes. The first mistake is that she didn't fully understand the opportunity before jumping in. She figured that the company would explode in popularity just as her old company did during the dot-com boom. Sally is essentially a helicopter salesperson. She knows this and hires Frank to do most of the work.

The next mistake Sally made was trying to slice the pie before it was baked. She carved off 10% and allocated it to Frank whom she hired on at half salary. Frank, seeing her wealth and past success, figured she knew what she was doing. Plus, she is a good salesperson and made Frank believe. It's okay to get Grunts to believe, that's the job. It's not okay to take advantage of them.

Sally, who also took a deferred salary, often brought up the sacrifice she was making to the other members of the team who were taking a salary. She thought they would work harder knowing how much she, herself, had on the line. However, because she had unfairly allocated the equity and kept the lion's share for herself everyone thought she sounded like a total prick. After all, she had already accumulated enough wealth to retire and she was still in the helicopter business.

Frank did his job, better than could be expected. He launched on time and hit the numbers. Sally was grateful to Frank and told him so- this is good treatment of a good employee. However, Sally got cold feet. She drastically overestimated the market. Times have changed so despite Frank's best efforts the company didn't have a chance of performing up to Sally's unrealistic expectations. She panicked and found, in Frank, a scapegoat.

She burned Frank by reneging on her deal. She pulled the rug out from under him by not expressing her concerns earlier and giving him a chance to correct. He was doing what she had asked and working hard. He deserved more warning. Next, she took back the equity that he had earned fair and square. Because he was terminated without cause, Frank had no choice in the matter and should expect to keep what he earned. Sally, who doesn't understand that pie grows, felt there was a finite amount of pie and that she needed to take it back so she could give it to her next victim. Otherwise she might have to give up hers (greed) or dilute the other participants, which would be fair in these circumstances.

Lastly, she forced Frank into an oppressive non-compete. In the event of termination with cause or resignation without cause a non-compete is appropriate. Companies should not provide incentive for a person to leave and create or join a competing firm.

However, in the case of resignation for good cause or termination without cause there should not be a non-compete. The individual has to find new work and they should not be hampered by a non-compete especially when the industry in which the company operates is likely to be the industry in which the person has the most contacts.

If you decide to cut someone loose for no reason you have to be willing to accept the consequences of doing so. Like I said before, you can't have your pie and eat it too. Non-competes are commonplace these days and largely unenforceable. However, just because companies use them doesn't make them right. They are only fair in certain circumstances.

The Case of:

PhoneMatcherator.com, LLC- Redux

Let's take a look at how this same story would have unfolded if Sally used a Grunt Fund:

Frank and Sally decided to use a Grunt Fund to start the company.

They decided to pay Frank a salary of $100,000 and used the following calculation to set a GHRR for Frank at $100 per hour:

Base Salary	$	200,000
Less Current Comp	$	100,000
Times Two	$	200,000
Divided by 2000	$	100

In a Grunt Fund a company is entitled to buy back certain shares in the event of termination without cause or resignation with good cause. Sally agreed to severance payments that would buy back the equity based on how long Frank worked. Frank understood that he would lose rights to equity if he left for no reason or was fired.

Sally also took a salary of $200,000 but she agreed to accept pie instead of cash giving her a GHRR of $200 per hour:

Base Salary	$	200,000
Less Current Comp	$	-
Times Two	$	400,000
Divided by 2000	$	200

When Sally began to worry that the company wouldn't be the overnight sensation that she had dreamed about and, on a whim, she terminated Frank without cause. Frank was shocked.

But because Frank was terminated without cause he was able to retain the pie had had earned. Sally bought back some of the pie with the company's cash as they had originally agreed, but Frank was treated fairly and the other team members knew it.

Sally was able to find a replacement for Frank, Ryan. Ryan started right away in the Grunt Fund and the team rallied around the him because they trusted Sally's judgment and there was still momentum in the company.

PhoneMatcher.com Survives

Using a Grunt Fund, Sally was able to avoid costly lawyers and accountants and focus on running the company. She and Frank had an honest relationship and they built a culture of trust.

Sally still got cold feet, but the Grunt Fund allowed her to change her mind and terminate Frank fairly. The other employees knew the rules of the Grunt Fund and saw that everything was fair and square. When Ryan came on board he was able to hit the ground running in the same trusting environment.

The Case of:

Lake Shark Ventures, LLC

Business incubators and accelerators seem to be exploding in popularity. At their core, they allow older, more experienced entrepreneurs tap the passion and energy of younger, less experienced entrepreneurs who need the help. Of course, most of them wouldn't sum up their business vision like that, but when you look at them from the outside that's exactly what's happening and I think it's great. When I was a budding entrepreneur wanting to change the world it would have been nice to have some office space, a good internet connection, some spending money and a little gray-haired advice.

Now that my own hair is turning gray, I find that I'm spending a lot of time providing advice (and sometimes spending money) to younger entrepreneurs. It's good for my ego (it makes me feel relevant), but I want to get paid! A

Grunt Fund can provide a way for mentors and advisors to benefit from the time they spend with start-up companies.

Lake Shark Ventures, LLC is a consulting company that is also a business incubator. The company offers early-stage start-up companies extremely reduced rates in exchange for a slice of the pie using a Grunt Fund.

Additionally, a group of affiliated professionals (Mentor-Grunts) spend time with the start-up portfolio companies offering advice and working on projects also in exchange for pie.

As you might imagine, things can get pretty complicated with a lot of different people working on a project. Plus, nobody likes the prospect of having to dole out equity to every Tom, Dick and Harry that provides some advice.

It is for this reason that Lake Shark has set up one single Grunt Fund to hold all the pie earned by the various contributors no matter what company the individuals spent time with.

It's sort of like a Grunt Fund that holds pie from other Grunt Funds. That way, when there is a liquidation event in any of the companies everyone who participated in the incubator benefits, even if they didn't actually spend time on the company that made money. (Stay with me on this....)

In an incubator setting the objective is to provide concrete incentive to individuals to spend time helping *all* the portfolio companies. When an individual spends an hour with one and a couple hours with another and another hour here and one there, the pie they earn is so small it's meaningless.

Moreover, when it comes time to allocate real equity no company wants to dole out small shares to a bunch of absentee owners who only spent a few hours on the project.

The Grunt Fund solves both problems. Here is how it works:

Step One: The company creates their own Grunt Fund, pie earned by advisors and mentors in this fund is held by Lake Shark Ventures

For example, Lake Shark has a start-up called Bug Supper, they make bug-tracking software. When the founder of Bug Supper and the Bug Supper team works on the company they each earn pie in the Bug Supper Grunt Fund. Additionally, when Lake Shark also provides inputs like office space, IT support, supplies and other items that help the business they also earn pie in the Bug Supper Grunt Fund.

However, the *time* that Lake Shark mentors and advisors spend on Bug Supper goes into another Grunt Fund that holds the pie from the Bug Supper Grunt Fund. Think of this as a "shared" Grunt Fund

Step Two: Lake Shark advisors and mentors track their time to the company, but earn pie in the shared Grunt Fund.

When someone outside the core team spends time advising, mentoring, freelancing, consulting or doing other work they log their time to the both the Bug Supper Grunt Fund and to the shared Grunt Fund.

For example, let's say Johan spends 10 hours at a GHRR of $200 per hour working with the Bug Supper team. The shared Grunt Fund earns a theoretical $2,000 in pie. Johan earns a theoretical $2,000 in the shared Grunt Fund.

Over time, lots of people come in and out of Lake Shark Ventures providing all sorts of good advice. They start five new companies, each with their own Grunt Fund. All the time that people dedicated to the various projects has created a shared Grunt Fund worth $100,000. Johan, who has dedicated over 100 hours on various projects, has earned a theoretical $25,000 in the shared Grunt Fund or ¼ of the total pie. He only spent 10 hours with Bug Supper, however. Other people spent more time so the total pie earned by all the people in the shared Grunt Fund is equal to 20% of the Bug Supper Grunt Fund.

Lake Shark, through its inputs of cash, rent and supplies, has earned another 20% of the Bug Supper Pie.

Step Three: When there is a liquidation event the members of the shared Grunt Fund receive a percentage equal to how much pie they earned.

One day Bug Supper is acquired by a

competitor for $1,000,000 cash. Everyone is elated. It's a cash offer so shareholders can take cash out of the company. Here is how it is distributed:

Participant	Pie	Dollars
Bug Supper Team	60%	$600,000
Lake Shark	20%	$200,000
Shared Grunt Fund	20%	$200,000

Because Johan is a 25% pie-holder in the shared Grunt Fund he receives $50,000 in cash. Likewise, the other participants in the shared Grunt Fund get checks equal to their own percentages.

It is true that Johan received more money than he would have if he had earned pie directly in Bug Supper's Grunt Fund, but he was spending lots of time with other portfolio companies that may cash in someday in which case others will be rewarded for his hard work.

Bug Supper loved this concept because they received all sorts of help from a lot of people, but they didn't have to pass out small shares to a lot of people. So, when the buyer's came-a-knockin' they found an intact pie and an easy transaction.

From time to time Lake Shark starts new shared Grunt Funds to hold pie for new groups of companies. A shared Grunt Fund works best when it holds pie for just a few companies. Remember, when the pie gets too big incremental hours don't add up to much and the motivation of adding more time dips.

Lake Shark uses the shared Grunt Fund model to manage small cash investments as well. Investors earn pie in the shared Grunt Fund which in turn earns pie in the company Grunt Funds when it disperses the cash. This allows them to create their own crowd-sourcing option for their start-ups.

Not everybody participates in the shared Grunt Fund. Sometimes people will spend enough time with a project that they will become part of the core team. In these cases they get a slice of the company pie instead of the shared Grunt Fund pie. When they leave the shared Grunt Fund they are essentially resigning without cause and are treated as such (see way above). The time that they forfeit from the shared Grunt Fund is gained in the company's Grunt Fund.

Other people don't participate in the shared Grunt Fund because they receive other value such as access to potential clients. Or maybe their time commitment is so nominal that it's not worth tracking.

At Lake Shark everyone is happy because they all have a mechanism for providing inputs that is fair and relatively easy to manage.

Too often incubators and accelerators are run like non-profit organizations. That's fine if they are incubating non-profit companies, but most of them are not. Most of the companies being incubated or accelerated have aspirations for world domination. The people who help them should participate in the rewards that are later reaped.

Lake Shark thrives by providing a stable work environment for passionate entrepreneurs and a means for experts to benefit from their inputs.

Lake Shark

Your Case Study

If you have a story that you think would make an interesting case study please let me know at mike@slicingpie.com. Would be happy to speak to you about your case and write it up for the SlicingPie.com blog or a new chapter in the book!

Getting Started

The nice thing about starting a company with a Grunt Fund is that you can start right now. You don't have to wait for anything, just start tracking your time and the other inputs.

Tomorrow, when you are trying to hire a new software developer for no money just tell him about your Grunt Fund and how you are all working together to build something.

When you are approaching suppliers that you can't pay, tell them you will pay them in pie by treating the cost of the services or products they provide like a cash contribution to your effort.

Grunt Funds are a clean, easy and quick way to start tapping the future equity of your company.

When you have questions or comments or ideas, please visit me at **www.SlicingPie.com**. I will answer your questions and provide more examples and furnish you with some nice spreadsheets for tracking things and I'll even post some links to some online tools that can help get you started.

Now that you've got the tools, go!

Free Upgrades

This is Version 2.3. From time to time I will release updated versions of Slicing Pie that incorporate new ideas and feedback from my readers. As a purchaser of this book you are eligible for free upgrades when they are available.

Free E-Upgrades for Life
To register for Free Upgrades of Slicing Pie for life visit **SlicingPie.com/upgrade** or scan the code.

Enter the code "islicepie"

Slicing Pie: the Game (yep, there's a game)

To help you and your cofounders better understand the impact of a dynamic equity split play the Slicing Pie board game! It's fun for all ages!

Slicing Pie Board Game
To learn more about the Slicing Pie board game visit
SlicingPie.com/game or scan the code.

Enter the code "pieplay"

The End

About the Author

Mike Moyer is a professional entrepreneur who has started companies from scratch, joined start-up companies, helped others start companies, raised millions of dollars of start-up capital and helped sell start-up companies.

He has worked in a variety of industries ranging from vacuum cleaners, to motor home chassis, to fine wine.

Mike has a MS in Integrated Marketing Communication from Northwestern University and an MBA from the University of Chicago. He teaches Entrepreneurship at both universities.

Mike is also the author of How to Make Colleges Want You and Trade Show Samurai. Mike lives in Lake Forest, Illinois with his wife and two kids (three kids after May, 2013), and the Lizard of Oz.

Talk to Mike

Please feel free to reach out to me with any questions, comments or concerns. Or, as I promised before, if this wasn't the best start-up funding advice you have ever received I will happily refund your money.

Email:	Mike@SlicingPie.com
Phone:	(773) 426-6353
Twitter:	@GruntFunds
Facebook:	facebook.com/mikedmoyer
LinkedIn:	linkedin.com/in/mikemoyer/
Website:	SlicingPie.com
	MikeMoyer.org

Special Thanks to individuals who provided important feedback that helped make me make Slicing Pie better!

Jacob Babcock   Gant Laborde
Johan Bartholf   Ryan McGeary
Chuck Bukrey   David Mittereder
Clint Costa   Alex Moseson
Alejandro Gomez

Release Notes: Version 2.3

Thank you to those who provided feedback and edits to earlier versions of this book. I have updated the book and have created this version 2.3. In this release I've added the following:

1. Updated dedication (because we had a new baby)

2. QR Codes that link to A La Mode topics

3. Grunt Glossary (please let me know if I should add other terms)

4. A variety of graphical and grammatical edits

5. The concept of a **Grunt Daily Resource Rate** (GDRR) with a chart on page 61

6. A note about **milestones** on page 67

7. A recommendation for a maximum GHRR on page 69

8. The introduction of the concept of the **"Well"** on page 72

9. More detail on how to value and provide appropriate rewards for ideas and **intellectual property** on page 83

10. A new chapter about how to **retrofit** the model to existing companies on page 131

11. An updated chapter (with a new title: "**Legalize It**") on legal issues you will want to discuss with your lawyer on page 145

12. Some new drawings of pies and Grunts

13. A new cartoon at the end

This list is not comprehensive, but hopefully it will help previous readers get acclimated to the new version quicker!

Please don't hesitate to provide additional feedback for future versions!

Grunt Glossary

Fat Grunt: A person who has more than his or her fair share of the equity relative to other participants.

Grunt: a person who works in a startup doing whatever it takes to make the company a success.

Grunt Hourly Resource Rate or **GHRR**: the theoretical value of one person's time relative to another person's time. It is not an actual value, it is used to calculate an individual's percent of the pie.

Pie: The equity in a company or a Promise to Issue Equity. Not all companies need to grant actual equity in order for this to work.

Skinny Grunt: A person who has less than his or her fair share of the equity relative to other participants.

Theoretical Base Value or TBV: because start-up companies are assumed to have no actual value in a Grunt Fund we use theoretical values with allow us to understand how important one contribution is relative to another contribution. The TBV is the sum off all the theoretical values of all contributions from all participants. It is used to calculate an individual's percent of the pie.

Well: a financing tool for a Grunt Fund where an investor provide cash in the form of a loan, the cash converts to pie at the 4x rate as it is used.

Leave a Review

Slicing Pie on Amazon.com

If you liked Slicing Pie, please leave a review on Amazon.com, I would really appreciate it! Scan the code to link to the review page.

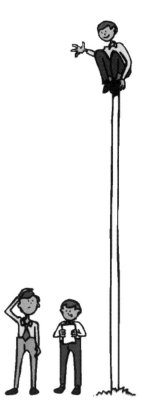

This Grunt Fund thing looks good, but I'm still going to have to run it up the flagpole for approval...

Made in the USA
San Bernardino, CA
09 August 2014